BUCKJUMPERS, GOBBLERS AND CLAUDS

BUCKJUMPERS GOBBLERS

AND

CLAUDS

*a lifetime on
Great Eastern and LNER
footplates*

Jim Hill

BRADFORD BARTON

ISBN 0 85153 396 5
copyright © Jim Hill 1981
set and printed by CTP Ltd for Top Link Ltd
for the publishers
D. BRADFORD BARTON LTD
Trethellan House · Truro · England

BD9474

CONTENTS

CHAPTER ONE

Joining the Great Eastern

ALTHOUGH IT IS now almost seventy years ago, I can well remember the day in 1913 when I went to see my boss in the London office where I was working as office boy, to give in my notice. He looked at me in amazement when I told him that I was leaving to join the Great Eastern Railway as an engine cleaner, with my ambitions set on ultimately becoming a driver. He regarded me with an incredulous expression and after a pause, asked how long I thought I would stand the job.

"Look in the looking-glass, lad, and think of yourself firing an express engine" was his comment!

I admit that I was a trifle skinny – and even now, over sixty-seven years later, I am still only 5'6" tall. But I was not to be dissuaded even when, somewhat mockingly, the boss said that he would keep my job open for me for one month!

I hadn't been really satisfied with my career since leaving school at the age of fourteen. My first job was in a solicitor's office in the area that I lived, Enfield Town, on the north-east edge of London. I had been dismissed from that job after only a year for fighting with the chief clerk!

At home I was variously known as Ed, Ted or even Eddie. It was my sister Eva – the school teacher – who first took me to school and put my name down on the register as Edwin James instead of James Edwin. Now, however, I was following in my father's footsteps; he was a signalman on the Great Eastern, at Enfield Town signalbox at the terminus of the very busy suburban line from Liverpool Street, the main station and headquarters of the railway.

There was much in common between being an engineman and a signalman, as both require an alert mind and a strong back. The locomotive fireman had a more arduous job and in the early years of this century it was generally considered that footplatemen needed more brawn than brains.

To the casual onlooker, the fireman's task looked to be a heavy one and a beginner rapidly found out just how heavy a task it was: just shovelling coal is child's play compared with having to do this on a real, live, kicking locomotive, trying to get each shovel-full through a hole, less than two feet wide, and onto a pre-determined spot on the grate.

The railways of my youth were almost as far removed from the railways of today as are the horse and cart from the modern jet-airliner. The railways in the major cities were beginning to feel the pinch of competition from the then modern electric tramways. But outside these main centres the railway was often the only means of land transport. Corridor trains, restaurant carriages and sleeping cars were a comparatively recent innovation to be found only on the principal express trains.

The Great Eastern Railway ran from Liverpool Street station to the edge of the City of London and extended its tentacles to all corners of East Anglia. In its early days in the 1860s it had to struggle to survive; at one point things were so bad that engines and rolling stock bore metal plates proclaiming to which of the railway's creditors they belonged! However, the G.E.R. was fundamental in the development of the London suburbs which sprang up along the banks of the river Lea – Tottenham, Edmonton, Enfield, Leyton, Walthamstow, and later, Chingford.

Gradually the railway started to pull round, reaching its most prosperous period in the years leading up to the Great War. An important factor had been the opening of the line from March to Peterborough in 1882, jointly with the Great Northern Railway, providing the G.E.R. with lucrative coal traffic from the north.

The Great Eastern was a very good employer: pay and conditions of that time were better than those of most British railways. It had been the first to introduce pension schemes for employees; it gave part-paid holidays; and on the whole, wages were higher, so much so in fact that when the G.E.R. was amalgamated with the London & North Eastern in 1923 there was a long period of stagnation on the late G.E.R. whilst the other lines caught up as regards wages.

However, the Great Eastern had none of the glory of other railways such as the London & North Western, the Great Northern or the Great Western with their crack express trains. The G.E.R. went about its business quietly but with great efficiency, transporting its passengers about East Anglia, to the continent via Harwich, or simply getting many thousands of people to and from the City each day. The commuter traffic was a principal feature of the G.E.R.'s operations – the densest ever worked by steam power anywhere in the world.

To operate all these services the G.E.R. had built up a stud of very efficient and highly standardised locomotives, the vast majority being designed and constructed in the company's works at Stratford. These works had been established by one of the Great Eastern's predecessors, the Eastern Counties Railway, in 1847. At that time Stratford was the junction of the Eastern Counties with the Northern & Eastern Railway, the E.C.R. going to Colchester, and the N. & E.R. striking northwards to Bishops Stortford and ultimately to Cambridge. In those bad old days, a man was stationed at the junction with a chain which he would string across the E.C.R. line when a N. & E.R. train was expected, and *vice versa*, to prevent any possible trespass of one company's engine upon the line of the other! The works at Stratford rapidly grew to become the focal point for building and maintaining locomotives as well as rolling stock of the G.E.R., although the wagon works had been moved a mile or two northwards to Temple Mills before the turn of the century. Because of the dense suburban traffic and consequently the large numbers of engines required to work it, Stratford was the largest locomotive shed in Britain, with an allocation of around 400 engines. Of these, roughly a quarter were sub-shedded at subsidiary depots, such as Enfield, Wood Street and Hertford, Ilford, Millwall, Epping and so on.

By the time that I was sent to Stratford to do my initial training, the locomotive and carriage works were on the east side of the old Cambridge line, whilst the main running shed and other works buildings covered the area inside the loop of tracks which by-passed Stratford station.

The year before I joined the Great Eastern Railway, A. J. Hill – no relation of mine – had become the Locomotive Superintendent. The majority of the locomotives had been built during the periods of office of James and Stephen Holden, father and son, dating back nearly thirty years to 1885. For the principal expresses, the new 1500 4–6–0s were used, the first having been built in 1911. But most of the express work fell to the famous 'Claud Hamilton' inside-cylinder 4–4–0s of which there were over a hundred in service. Some of these were originally built to burn oil as fuel on James Holden's patent system. This was an early example of conservation; his fuel oil was a by-product of the production of oil-gas for carriage lighting, the G.E.R. having its own oil-gas works at Stratford. Previous to its use for firing locomotives, the oil-tar residue was dumped in the Channelsea River which flowed through the Stratford complex. Holden found that by heating this tarry waste, and spraying it into the firebox of engines by steam pressure it would burn very successfully. However, with the perfection of the internal combustion in the first decade of the century, and consequent rise in the demand for oil, the price rose to such an extent so as to nullify any cost advantage over coal.

For suburban traffic there were over a hundred small 0–6–0 tank engines – the 'Buckjumpers'; forty 0–4–4 tanks and a large class of 2–4–2 radial tanks. These were known as 'Gobblers', an unkind nick-name that had stuck since the first thirty engines were built in 1884 and were found to be heavy on fuel consumption. The Joy valve-gear with which they were fitted was replaced by Stephenson's gear early in their careers, curbing their appetite for coal, but the soubriquet remained.

For goods work there were the well-loved 'Little Goods' 0–6–0 tender engines. There were nearly three hundred of these simple, ruggedly constructed machines spread all over the G.E.R. system and they were truly maids-of-all-work; go-anywhere, do-anything engines, many fitted with continuous brakes to enable them to work excursion train specials when the need arose. Such was the quality of the Stratford workmanship that a handful of these locomotives still remained at work when steam was replaced by diesel on the majority of the G.E. lines in September 1962. Assisting the 'Little Goods' was a class of more modern and heavier locomotives, the '1150' 0–6–0s.

The largest of the passenger tank engines were the C32 class 2–4–2 tanks. These handled the longer distance passenger trains on the Southend lines, or to Bishops Stortford, whilst others worked the long cross-country lines of the system. There was also a small class of diminutive 2–4–2 Ts, the 'Crystal Palace' tanks, so-called because of their large cabs with massive windows. One of these was fitted as an auto push-pull during the First World War and ran between White Hart Lane and Cheshunt, with my cousin Charlie Whipps often taking turns as driver.

Together with these there were also a few engines of other classes, not so often seen in the London area by my time; among these were the T19 2–4–0 and 4–4–0 express engines, rebuilt from James Holden's original T19 class 2–4–0s of 1886 with larger boilers. The rebuilt 2–4–0s were peculiar-looking machines, the large boilers giving them a hunched-up appearance, hence the nick-name 'Humpty Dumpties'. The rebuilt 4–4–0s were better looking, both types working mainly on the joint line from March to Peterborough, or in the country districts.

There were also one hundred 2–4–0 tender engines for mixed traffic, known as the 'Intermediates', which were also employed mainly on the country lines. One of these survived to become the last 2–4–0 tender engine in service in Britain and is now preserved in the National Railway Museum at York, along with one of the 'Buckjumper' 0–6–0s, No.87.

When I joined the Great Eastern, their engines were always well turned-out. All those fitted with continuous train brakes were painted deep ultramarine blue with black borders and red lining; goods engines were black with red lining, whilst shunting tanks were plain black without lining. Every engine, irrespective of its job, sported polished brass and metalwork, vermilion coupling-rods and carried polished brass numberplates with vermilion backgrounds.

In those days there was no such thing as work study: the locomotive needed a two-man crew, one to drive it and one to feed the boiler. These intrepid men were merely provided with a platform to stand on at the back end of the boiler, and covered with a shelter or cab. It kept the rain out and the wind, when running, but was decidedly draughty. The crew had to stand on the footplate with searing heat from the fire on one side and an icy draught on the other. However, the Great Eastern was foremost in attempting to provide better protection for its engine crews by providing large, spacious side-window cabs on the more modern engines. The discomfort of working a train, tender-first, over any distance, facing all the elements, especially freezing fog, had to be experienced to be believed.

The controls were dotted around the cab in the most economical manner to give the most direct operation to whatever appliance they controlled. In those days the crew were not supposed to sit down whilst the engine was in motion, so it mattered little if they had to hop about the cab to operate the controls. The regulator was in the boiler centre, the reversing wheel needed a step back to operate it, the damper controls stuck out through the floorboards, and so on. On the 'Little Goods' class for example, when running backwards, there was no power operation of the sanding equipment: sand had to be poured down a funnel under the driver's seat!

The only attempt made to group the controls together was to put those for the driver on the right-hand side of the cab, and those for the fireman on the left, mainly because of tradition. Most of the signals and platforms were on the left side of the track and the driver's position on the right was thus of little hindrance in the early days when locomotive boilers were of small enough diameter to see over or round. But in the years after the turn of the century, engine boilers had become longer, larger, and pitched at a greater height above the rails, obscuring the driver's view. It was not until the amalgamation of the Great Eastern into the L.N.E.R. that the driver's place on the footplate was changed to the more logical position on the left, and then only on new engines. This, of course, forced the fireman to fire from the opposite position, which is easier said than done.

This then, in brief was the Great Eastern Railway on that day in 1913 when I signed on for the first time at Stratford as an engine cleaner, the first step on the long ladder of promotion to engine driver.

CHAPTER TWO

War Intervenes

THERE WERE FOUR stages of promotion between joining the railway service and reaching one's goal of becoming an engine driver. The first stage was as an engine cleaner, and this was followed by becoming a 'passed' cleaner, that is a cleaner who had become adequately trained to act as fireman when required. Then followed promotion to fireman, followed by 'passed' fireman – a fireman who could act as driver when required.

The cleaner, besides his primary task of cleaning engines, also had to use his time to learn their different parts and their function, as well as to familiarise himself with the various types of locomotive that he would come across in his career. Labour was cheap and the hours long. In those days, great importance was placed on having not only clean but polished locomotives to haul all trains. The drivers themselves, especially those on the top link express turns, were very fastidious in ensuring that their steeds were in as good a condition externally as they were mechanically, and woe betide any cleaning gang that skimped its work.

After my initial training period at Stratford I became a fully paid-up engine cleaner at Enfield Town shed. The general rule was that unless there was a rush job on, four men would be assigned to clean a tank engine and six to a tender engine. At Enfield we had all tanks, and, with the exception of the shed engines, they were all cleaned at night. The shed engines, generally three in number, were those laid up for repairs or boiler wash-out, and so on. Each gang of four cleaners was assigned to regular engines so that the foreman knew who to blame for any faults. However, if there was a spare engine in place of the regular one, the same gang of four were allocated to the job.

A tank engine was divided into four parts for cleaning: the tanks and wheels, either side; the boiler, footplate and smokebox, including the dome, chimney and safety-valves and the attached brass fittings; and finally the motion beneath the engine, or 'the works', including the axles and the inside of the frames. We picked our individual jobs by the toss of a coin and if the engine was available we started.

For the night's work each cleaner was given twelve wet washed cloths, sometimes called 'khaki', which were laid on any available warm boiler to dry. In addition we were issued with two swabs – washed cloths soaked in cleaning oil – a lump of tallow for cleaning the smokebox and chimney, a brick swab for brass cleaning, and two new sponge cloths. These latter were looked after like gold dust.

Our hours on night work were from 10pm to 8am. The last engine cleaned was to be manned by its crew at 5.30am, so between then and 8am we had the job of picking up the clinker that was lying about the loco yard. Other jobs to be done included cleaning the enginemen's mess-room, sweeping and cleaning the engine pits in the shed, and cleaning the shed itself. Two of us also had to go calling-up enginemen who were on duty between 3 and 5.30am.

One other job which was carried out twice a week fell to the strongest-looking amongst us. At 4am he had to catch the first train of the morning from Enfield Town to Stratford, changing at Bethnal Green, carrying a tarpaulin sack full of all the oily cloths and rags used by the drivers, fitters and cleaners. These he delivered to Stratford where they were processed by the gas works to make oil-gas for carriage lighting: there was certainly no waste on the Great Eastern! The cleaner then had to return to Enfield carrying a similar sack full of clean washed cloths.

Our duties left a little time for the odd prank or two: a favourite trick on New Year's Eve was to wedge pieces of coal in the engine whistles so that once started, the whistle would go on issuing a piercing shriek until someone managed to silence it! Another joke involved climbing the water-tower unseen whilst some unsuspecting fireman was watering his engine. By standing on the operating lever, the water-valve could be prevented from closing with the result that when the victim removed the filling bag from the tank-filler he got an unscheduled shower. Nor was it difficult to prepare the odd snack during the night: backing onto the shed in those days was a field where potatoes were growing. A quick expedition would procure a few likely-sized potatoes, which were then placed in any handy safety-valve casing to cook.

Within a year of my joining the Railway came the outbreak of war, but at first this did not make much impression on day-to-day life and things carried on much as before. Early in 1915 the first of a new class of large 0–6–2 tanks was introduced for work on suburban services. She was No.1000, and whilst running-in was painted in 'photographic grey'. But events overtook her, for she was never to wear the deep blue livery as did her sister No.1001, when she entered service a month or two later.

No.1001 was fitted with a superheater, a new innovation for a suburban engine, and trials were carried out to compare her with No.1000, which was a saturated engine. However, the war in Europe prevented any further developments.

It was also early in 1915 that a notice was posted in Enfield Town depot asking for railwaymen to volunteer for service in the Railway Operating Division (R.O.D.) of the Royal Engineers. Myself and five others agreed to enlist, but only two of us turned up at the interview, and my companion failed the medical examination. However, there were ten of us from the Stratford District who had to report for training at the Longmoor Depot of the Royal Engineers shortly after. One thing which quite impressed all of us was that we were to retain our seniority dates for promotion on the railway when we were demobbed, should we return to the Company's service.

Training at Longmoor consisted solely of square bashing and physical training, no mention being made of railways all the time that I was there. To our surprise, in September we were returned to civilian life and I found myself cleaning, back at Enfield Town. However, in January 1916 I was instructed again to report to Longmoor for overseas duty and within a short while I was en route across the Channel with thousands of others to join the War.

We spent our first night in Boulogne at a place known as the 'rat hole' – a brewery warehouse I believe. The next day we were taken to Audruicq, then the headquarters of the R.O.D. I spent a week there engine cleaning and then eventually about a dozen of us were picked out and told to report to Poperinge, which according to the grape vine was under shell-fire.

However, on arrival there was no shell-fire to greet us, although the station and its environs were very much the worse for wear. I had initially thought that transfer to Poperinge was a piece of bad luck, as Audruicq was well behind the firing lines, but a few months later we heard that the latter had been heavily bombarded with the R.O.D. suffering heavy casualties.

Poperinge was in Belgium, and the story went that when the Germans had advanced, engines stationed there had been pushed into the Yser canal to stop them falling into enemy hands. Upon the subsequent re-capture of Ypres by the British, the Royal Engineers had fished them out again and handed them over to the R.O.D. We under-20s were put to cleaning duties again on the Belgian locos. These were all 0–6–0 tenders with Westinghouse brakes as on the G.E.R., but equipped with equalising brake valves, a refinement we didn't have back home. They also had Gresham & Craven injectors, which took some time to get used to, also a wheel in the fireman's corner to operate the rocking grate for cleaning the fire. After a period of having been in the canal, this wheel needed something of a superman to operate it . . .

Poperinge was on the railway line from Calais to Ypres and Passchendaele Ridge. From Calais the only stations that concerned us were Audruicq, St. Omer, Hazebrouck, Borre Camp, Castres, Godewaersvelde, Adeele, Remy Hospital Camp, Poperinge, Vlamertinge and Ypres. The French enginemen used to work as far as Hazebrouck and it was here that some of the British engines were stored. This was an R.O.D. depot until Borre Camp was formed, which ultimately embraced Poperinge depot in 1916.

At Borre too, the G.E.R. breakdown crane was stationed, always in steam and at the ready, in a short siding by the side of the Camp loco office. A tale about this comes to mind: my duty was as caller-up at night with two other men, working three shifts. One of our jobs was to look after the fire and water for the crane, and in freezing weather to open the steam cocks to the valves. All the controls were left in neutral by the crane driver. On this particular night, the other caller-up could not resist the temptation to have a go and, after trial and error, succeeded in swinging the jib over the main line. He could not however, fathom out how to get it back, so his first urgent job was to go and get the crane driver out of bed to do the necessary before any trains passed by on the main line.

Castres station, near Borre, was at the foot of a steep incline and always had a banking engine in attendance. This was generally a very old Belgian engine with characteristic square chimney and a huge firehole door that was in two parts which opened over the entire width of the firebox. There was no real brake in the accepted sense, this being effected by some means of water compression, I believe. Between here and Godewaersvelde was the border of France and Belgium. At Abeele, running east, was a branch-line laid out by our engineers to Ouderdom and the infamous Hill 60. At Ouderdom locomotives could take water: a Merryweather pump was installed there manned by a R.E. sergeant, one Alf Abbott of whom more later.

Remy Hospital was next down the line followed by Poperinge, normally our terminus. In emergencies however, we were called upon to work an armoured engine and on one dark night, required to creep up to Vlamertinge, with necessary instructions to keep the engine quiet and not to open the firehole door whilst taking fresh troops to the front or when returning with the wounded.

Troop trains, as well as those for the wounded in the early stages of the war, were composed of old French coaching stock, far worse than anything on the G.E.R. – and some of that was bad enough. The leave trains on this sector of the front were ordinary long-wheelbase open trucks with a roof fitted, and equipped with a slow-combustion stove, similar to the pattern used in goods brakes.

At Poperinge, our living quarters consisted of railway cattle-trucks fitted with bunks. This train was stationed between two stacks of British coal, whitewashed army-style. Nearby was a dug-out shelter for our use during shelling.

Our work at first was solely to meet the army's requirements, working trains as far as Hazebrouck where French enginemen took charge. It was here that I learned what a lead plug was for: amongst the British engines kept at Hazebrouck there were several 'Little Goods' 0–6–0s from the G.E.R. Enginemen not of the Great Eastern Railway were very apprehensive about working on one of these engines because they had no fusible lead plugs. These are hollow plugs filled with lead, and let into the firebox crown; should the water level in the boiler drop below the acceptable limit, and uncover the firebox crown, the lead would melt, spraying steam into the inner firebox. This would not just dampen the fire, but often put it out, preventing the copper inner shell of the fire box from collapsing.

Conversely, the ex-G.E.R. men amongst us were just as windy about taking charge of a non-G.E.R. engine for fear of 'dropping the plug'. The device was foreign to us, since none of our engines back home had them, and in the end, to keep the peace, the authorities had lead plugs fitted on 'washout days' to the ex-G.E.R. engines.

CHAPTER THREE

R.O.D. Experience

WITHIN A SHORT time I was made up to fireman, working on the British engines. During 1916 the depot at Borre became the main point for housing engines and men, embracing Hazebrouck and us at Poperinge.

At the same time the French must have asked for assistance in working their train services, so after tuition by the older enginemen we started working the other side of Hazebrouck, but still manning British locomotives. The passenger trains were equipped with Westinghouse brakes, as used on the G.E.R. and a few other British lines, the North Eastern among them.

About this time some new engines were sent to the front by the Dutch Government, a batch of large 4–6–4 tank engines built by Beyer, Peacock of Manchester and fitted with Westinghouse brakes. They caused quite a stir as to who should man them.

By now we were getting short of qualified drivers and firemen, and unknown to us, a notice was exhibited to the fighting forces asking for railwaymen among them to report to any R.O.D. depot. Even sewing-machine salesmen answered the call!

The test given to the volunteers was simple. An interviewer pointed to various parts of a locomotive and asked, "What's that for?" One of our sergeant-majors knew that Sergeant Alf Abbott at Ouderdom was an engine driver from the North Eastern Railway and had him brought to Borre: very peeved he was to have to leave his cushy but dangerous job not far from the front line. There he was looking after a Merryweather pump, supplying all steam engines needing water, road haulage or otherwise. He told me he was living in clover; he lived in a home-made dug-out, kept one or two chickens and even had a woman to cook his meals.

At Borre, Alf was given charge of one of the new Dutch 4–6–4 tanks and within a day or so I was booked as his fireman. Right from the start there existed a friendly atmosphere; he was slightly deaf, and with me having a sister with a similar affliction we understood each other. After a week he asked for me as his regular mate. There were fourteen of these tanks in all, numbered from 1 to 15, omitting 13 to thwart any bad luck. Ours was No. 10.

It was whilst working on these big tanks that my friendship with Syd Burgess started: he was a fireman on one of the others. That friendship lasted until he died in 1969, but I will return to Syd later.

These 4–6–4Ts were very capable machines, weighing 93 tons in working order, with driving wheels 6'⅞" in diameter and cylinders 20" diameter by 26" stroke. The boiler had a Belpaire firebox fitted with a Schmidt superheater, and provided steam at a pressure of 170lbs per sq. in.

The Schmidt superheater had been used at first on G.E.R. engines, and with this apparatus a damper was provided to protect the elements when coasting: when the regulator was opened, steam was supplied to a small cylinder on the smokebox side which opened the damper. When the regulator was shut, the damper closed by gravity. Gresham and Craven injectors were fitted, and a pet-pipe was attached to that on the fireman's side for watering the coal, whilst to the injector on the driver's side was attached a pipe running to the smokebox to damp down the ashes prior to their removal. A Wakefield mechanical lubricator was fitted for the valves and pistons: this was unusually mounted in the cab on the fireman's side. On these engines, the driver's side was on the left, so I had become well-used to firing on the right of the engine when returning to civil life.

The firebox of these tank engines had a drop-grate and the ashpan had two sliding doors. To change the water in the boiler, if a wash-out was overdue, there was a remote control handle on top of the tank which allowed the boiler to be blown down in safety whilst using the injector. The fire-irons were stored between the boiler and tanks, in the cab, and the bunker could be covered by hinged metal doors when travelling bunker first, preventing coal dust from blowing into the cab.

One of the finest assets of the 4–6–4 from our point of view was that the whole of the cab could be enclosed with sliding windows.

This was a blessing to us as we were sleeping on this engine in 1918 when the German advance took place and all engines that were in steam were moved towards Dunkirk.

With the rostering of regular crews to these engines, my work altered completely. Working ambulance trains was our chief occupation until more men of experience were found. By this time a chain of men was formed to work any train as required upon the Nord Railway, goods and passenger, and especially our own ambulance trains. When it was thought that these might be needed we were standing by, engine prepared ready for the word 'go'. It might be from, or to, anywhere.

When working ambulance trains, we were unofficially regarded as part of the staff: at each stop for loading and unloading, I would go back down the train to the cook house to see what was going. In return, we supplied them with all the hot water they required. An interesting point about these trains was that we carried a board with a large red cross on both sides of the smokebox, and to give 'Jerry' his due, we were never fired upon while working these trains.

Also at this time, the brass domes of these engines, which we lovingly polished with a substance known as 'Derby Paste' were painted over as they were becoming a landmark for the German Army.

It was on one of these ambulance runs that I became a real driver – unofficial of course. Alf spent a lot of his time, when on 'waiting orders' in the wet canteen, leaving me to hold the fort and do the necessary jobs that engine preparation entails.

I was attending to these duties when suddenly the orderly sergeant appeared to give Alf his orders and, failing to see him, the sergeant asked me to pass them on to him – work an ambulance train from Remy to Boulogne. By this time Alf was getting into a fighting mood with another sergeant, being very much the worse for the quantity of alcohol that he had imbibed. Thank goodness he recognised me and allowed me to lead him to the engine and help him aboard. In the heat he could hardly stand upright, let alone drive, so I settled him down on the floor of the cab between the bunker and fire-door. By straddling his prone body I was able to wield the shovel and move to either side as need arose . . .

In this way I managed to get the engine out of the depot with no-one the wiser and take it light to Remy to pick up an ambulance train. Here I contacted the guard and explained matters; luckily he was sympathetic. With the 'right away' we were off to Boulogne *via*

Calais. It was solely through Alf's tuition that I had attained confidence enough to fire and drive the engine by myself, since on normal days he would often let me stand in as driver. But on that night, it was rather tricky – firing over his body, maintaining steam and checking the signals, but by good fortune we had no stops.

After leaving Calais, I had Caffins bank to face, which meant that I had to shovel more coal. Until now Alf had not stirred, and I decided that it was time he returned to the land of the living: after much shouting and pushing, all to no avail, I poured half a bucket of cold water over his face. This had the desired result: he returned to consciousness, but took a while to come to his senses, sitting on the seat and looking around before he realised where he was. However, he soon took control and wanted to know what had happened; how he had got out of the canteen and onto the engine, and whether anyone had seen us. He was greatly relieved and thankful that no-one suspected anything.

We remained at Borre until the German advance of 1918 and not long after we had to evacuate the place. For this, all of the Borre engines were split into groups according to which British railway company they had come from. At Borre we had representatives of engines from the Great Eastern, Great Central, Great Western, Great Northern, North Eastern and Lancashire & Yorkshire railways, as well as one or two American Baldwin 'spider type', plus two of our 4–6–4 tanks. These engines were all worked to R.O.D. depots away from the shelling.

Ultimately, our group of engines were housed on a loop line at Hondingham, the other side of St. Omer, and this became our main depot for coal, water and running repairs. Accommodation was spartan to say the least: the enginemen's cookhouse and store were two vans. There was no sleeping accommodation, only the cabs of our engines. Luckily of course, our No.10 had its large closed-in cab. The others had the draughty open cabs of the more primitive machines. There was no rostering of work either, and the simple principle of 'last-in, last-out' settled the question of times on and off duty!

Each engine, when arriving back at the depot went to the rear of the line of engines and very gingerly coupled up. Failure to do this gently – smacking the buffers – resulted in a stream of lively abuse from the residents of the other engines! When leaving, each engine moved up to first position, drawing the others with it, the engines being left with their handbrakes off.

Strange to say, this system worked very well. We took our turn on light goods trains, but generally we were kept back for ambulance or passenger work. We also started working French passenger trains: this began with running the relief train for the coal miners at Noeux-les-Mines near the front lines at Bethune and Lillers. We also had two passenger trains to Boulogne; one *via* Calais, and the other *via* Lumbres and then on a single line to Boulogne. Owing to the gradients on this line we referred to it as 'going over the Alps'. All of these trains started from Hazebrouck. We had a French guard with the passenger trains, but an R.O.D. guard on the ambulance trains and short distance goods.

Much of our time on these trips was spent shunting before returning to Hazebrouck: whilst shunting I was generally the driver, and usually fireman as well on Alf's pay-day!

During the period that Alf and I were together, we always shared the rations that we drew from the stores, Alf's as for a sergeant and myself as a sapper. His numerous acquaintances from the wet canteen looked after him nicely as well, and sometimes he would board the engine as pleased as punch, with raw meat instead of the perpetual bully beef. 'R.O.D. 10' was, of course, fully equipped with improvised cooking facilities, ranging from a frying pan to a half-gallon can with a wire handle for a boil-up in the fire-box, Alf being the head chef.

On one occasion we were booked on a passenger train to Boulogne via Lumbres and Derves. During the trip, Alf was arranging the dinner menu, remarking that he knew of a field of potatoes near a certain signal, and added, "If only we had a cabbage to go with it." When we stopped at Derves we spotted an allotment near the end of the platform and, lo and behold, right beside our engine was a cabbage! Alf was soon trying to 'Parlez vous' with its owner, the station master. He asked, "How much?", but the station master drew the transaction to an untimely end by walking away.

Alf was not going to take no for an answer. As was usual on this route it was rather foggy, and this gave him an idea. He returned to the ground on the cabbage side of the engine, where the waste-water pipe of the injector was leaking steam. He kicked it, and then shouted to me to try and stop it by opening the steam cock and shutting it smartly.

"Try again," said Alf. "Leave it open longer this time." I did this several times and eventually lost sight of him among the clouds of billowing steam, that is until he climbed back into the cab clutching the cabbage! Needless to say we were not around to see the station master's face when he found the hole in the soil where his cabbage was supposed to be!

A further insight into Alf's character became evident in 1918 when Jerry made his final breakthrough. A fair number of civilians were still living at Hazebrouck and one of our jobs at this time involved working evacuation trains away from the danger area. On one occasion, the priests and various dignitaries were seeing all of the children put on board, some parents and teachers accompanying them and others saying goodbye.

Alf had to poke his nose in. He came hurrying up to our engine and proceeded to empty our tool locker of all of our food stores: bread, cheese, jam, cakes and some sweets sent from home; he distributed these amongst the passengers, bless his old heart.

He returned saying, "We can always get more where that came from, Jim boy. You should have seen their faces light up."

I hope that Alf explained to the beneficiaries which packets contained soap and which contained cheese – it was not always possible to tell in those days – owing to the heat of the engine.

A cooler driver than Alf there never was in those dangerous times. While working coal-miners trains to Noeux-les-Mines, just outside Lillers, we were running round the train for the return journey one day and a barrage of artillery fire started. A shell dropped close by our engine, shattering the windows and gauge-glasses. Alf calmly alighted, made sure that we were still on the road – and that the track was still there – checked that I was unhurt, and then drove the engine to the other end of the train like a bat out of hell. Although workable, No.10 never seemed to be quite the same again, but it still had the ability to scramble home.

The write-off of our R.O.D. 10 came towards the closing months of the war, when we had come to learn the French railway system much further from our home depot because of the shortage of local staff and engines. It was also towards the end of my partnership with Alf. We were working an ambulance train to Etaples where the locomotive depot was run in a very slip-shod way.

After our arrival and disposal of the train, we were instructed to take the engine to the coal road to get fuel and water for the return journey. The facilities and the mess rooms were scattered about the depot and nobody came with us as guide; we were told we should find a coalman at the wagon. In finding our way across the depot we noticed crossing a double line of sidings – or so we thought. There were no signals to help us, but we found the coalman waiting and set the engine for him to do his job and we got on with ours.

We were now ready to leave and as we departed the coalman remarked, "Keep your eyeballs wobbling going back!" Away we went, not really appreciating this farewell. But because the road was rocky, we crawled along to the engine sidings and the cook-house, a trip which we were in a moment to discover crossed the main line.

This was badly situated for visibility in both directions. We checked that the road was clear and kept the engine in motion; then, half-way across, a train appeared travelling round the bend at a good speed and was unavoidably going to clout us broadside on.

Alf could see what was going to happen, but did not know whether to reverse or keep going. He chose the latter and opened the regulator wide. However a collision was inevitable and we stopped with the other engine's buffers halfway into our tank. Water was cascading down and steam escaping with a continual roar until Alf closed the regulator.

The tank was now empty, with water everywhere. As the noise subsided, the language between the four of us could be heard, but the mud-slinging soon ended with the arrival of an officer, a sergeant and a red-cap.

Fortunately, no-one had been injured, but there was plenty of damage, not only to the locos, but to the rolling stock and track, and plenty of questions too. Not unexpectedly, as the other men were on their home ground, whilst we were strangers, they got their own version of the accident recorded first by the C.O.

We were then told to report to the orderly room with the red-cap as pilot. Alf didn't say much. We were immediately placed on open arrest pending an enquiry why we were crossing the main line without ensuring that the road was clear. Alf asked that the case be heard at our own depot, Malhove, near St. Omer. We had to work our booked train home, but with a pilot engine and armed guard on the footplate.

A day or two later the case came up for hearing. Alf was quite unconcerned and told me to answer truthfully any questions asked of me, saying that he would conduct his own defence. The charge was duly read out and Alf pleaded 'Not guilty', and was then asked to state the facts as he saw them.

I can recall Alf saying, "Sir, in hall my railway hexperience, I have never known a Main Line being crossed either by han engine or train without hany signals controlling the lines."

Our C.O. then questioned the prosecution about the lack of controls, and whether there was a shunter or pointsman controlling the crossing movements. He received a negative reply. We were then told to withdraw while they weighed the evidence. The subsequent result was 'case dismissed', with a warning to be more careful in future.

Within a month of this affair I was asked if I was prepared to take charge of an engine myself, with promotion to lance-corporal and increased pay. Much to Alf's disgust I accepted.

My first job was working a goods train to Abbeville with a 'Spider' class 'Baldwin', strong as an ox in brake power and hauling ability.

My experience with Alf Abbott stood me in good stead: his parting advice to me was, "Never be sorry, be careful." . . .

I myself heard the news of the armistice in 1918 whilst working a freight train at Lumbres with Alf on R.O.D. 10. Shortly afterwards we found ourselves closer to what had been the firing lines than we had ever been in daylight and I remember the journey vividly.

We were working a goods train from Hazebrouck to Poperinge and on our arrival an officer appeared and instructed us not to uncouple, but instead to carry on to Ypres and beyond. Alf wanted to return to our depot at Malhove, as by this time we had done more than our turn of duty, and made no reply to the officer, ignoring him completely.

The officer then asked me who my driver was, and I told him that Alf was a bit deaf, knowing that Alf had fully understood the order, nevertheless, and was playing for time to come up with an excuse. However, the order was duly repeated at a volume that even Alf could not ignore.

Alf then played his trump card, saying that he did not know the road and that he would need a pilotman. This stumped the officer for a moment, who then went into a huddle with a group of NCOs, but came back to us with the reply that a pilotman was not available and that we would have to make our way as best we could.

I had never been beyond Poperinge in daylight; Vlamertinge, Hellfire Corner and Passchendaele were just names to me, places passed in the dark. However, they were now revealed to me as piles of rubble, with the Yser Canal spreading itself among the shell-holes. I remember the haunting faces of the battleworn troops walking, almost zombie-like, along the track: each group had their own lookout, but each man had his own idea how far from the train was a safe distance. I recall one weary soldier staggering out of our way, hardly noticing our passage; the cab footsteps tore into his coat as we passed.

It was shortly after this that I was offered promotion to driver, and in the weeks before I was demobbed, just before Christmas 1918, I must have driven most types of British locomotives in France at the time.

Every railway enthusiast I know has his own idea which railway had the best locomotives, but from a professional point of view the 'Dean Goods' 0–6–0 tender engines of the Great Western took top marks all round. The only point which let them down was the cab, which was too exposed to the elements. They ran like sewing machines, with no knocks from big ends or side rods. The vacuum brake application handle had only three positions, 'large ejector', 'running' and 'application'. There was no small ejector on G.W. engines to maintain the vacuum when runnning. Instead there was a small piston operated by the motion; a very reliable arrangement I found. The injectors were also well designed and could be easily regulated to suit the working of the engine. The driver's side injector could really swamp water into the boiler.

My mention of Great Western engines brings to mind a tale told to me some years later by my cousin, Charlie Whipps, who was also a driver at Stratford. Charlie used to spend his holidays at Penzance. On his journey home he arrived at the station to catch the train up to London and noticed two fitters at the end of the platform with a trolley containing a connecting rod. Unlike G.E.R. locomotives, which had a collar and set-screws for adjusting any knock caused by wear on the bearings, the G.W.R. engines had only a bush.

Charlie introduced himself to these fitters as a fellow engineman and was soon engaged in conversation. To his amazement, he was told they were waiting to fit the connecting rod to the engine which was to work his train to Paddington! On the G.E., after fitting a new big-end bearing to an express engine, it was booked for goods work for at least a week until it was run-in; hence Charlie's surprise!

He asked the fitters how far they thought the driver would get before he required a new engine. The fitter then showed him two knobs of tallow, which he placed in the oil cups of the new connecting rod, saying that if they had even slightly melted by the time the train got to London, the fitters would be for the high jump.

Charlie spoke with the driver about this when the operation was taking place and later, at Paddington, the driver was waiting for

Charlie. When they looked in the oil-caps, the tallow was exactly the same as when put in at Penzance. . . .

My last job whilst serving in the R.O.D. was concerned with the handing-over of German locomotives to the Allies under the Reparations Agreements. I had the job of piloting these engines to their booked destinations from the various distribution centres. Generally they were moved in batches of three at a time, the leading engine being in steam with a German driver, a fireman and myself, plus a fireman on both of the two dead engines.

My orders were that I was to consider myself part of the crew and that the German driver was in overall charge. He was responsible for which fireman manned which engine, also for supervising the preparation and disposal of the locomotives. My job was to accompany them until the engines were handed over, as well as to see that signals and speed limits were adhered to, and to draw the rations from the R.T.O. at the various stations.

The German locomotives themselves seemed to be in much better condition than any we had in the R.O.D. Several of these engines were compounds – strange to me, but this was no worrry of mine, as the drivers were responsible for working them. I noticed that they often made use of the starting valve when the engine would not pull, admitting live steam into the low-pressure cylinder and giving more power.

CHAPTER FOUR

Back to Civilian Life

I RETURNED TO civil life late in 1918, and after a fortnight's leave reported to Stratford shed for a medical examination, just as though I was starting afresh. However, I retained my seniority date prior to Army service: this was the date that I first joined the railway, which was used to reckon seniority when promoted.

By this time, all the other men in my seniority group were regular firemen, and provision had to be made for me to take my rightful place in the rosters, as it had been agreed between the management and unions that every demobbed soldier returning to railway service should take the same position as though he had not enlisted. In addition, any back-payments would be decided by each ex-serviceman receiving the same wage as his next most junior man. I shall return to this later.

I was then put through the examination for 'passed' cleaner and fireman. In the normal course of events, these two examinations would be taken some years apart, the first just to the stage of 'passed' cleaner. This would be the first occasion that a cleaner would be allowed on the footplate of a live steam engine, which he would do full of confidence, thinking he knows all about locomotives. Upon picking up the shovel he would rapidly realise just how little he really did know.

The next stage in the engineman's career was to be made up to full fireman, then to 'passed' fireman and so able to act as driver when required, and finally to driver.

Whilst a fireman, he was expected to learn a multitude of facts about the lines he worked over: the stations, signal boxes, level crossings, gradients, signals, water troughs and a host of other things beside his prime function of stoking the boiler. His first jobs would be on shunting engines, moving through the various links of local goods, long distance goods, local passenger and so on, up to firing on top link expresses.

He would then come up for promotion to driver, whereupon it would be back to the bottom again, starting on shunting engines and working up to the top. Promotion depended a lot on filling dead men's shoes and it was general for a man to be in his forties before becoming a driver: at small depots, where promotion was slow, it could take a good deal longer.

In my case, however, I passed the examination for passed cleaner and fireman in two weeks and applied for and was subsequently accepted for a firing vacancy at Enfield Town. What a change after three years in the Army! Then followed two difficult years, firing to a driver who was a bundle of nerves, continually grumbling, and who made my life a misery.

It was important for a driver and fireman to work regularly together in order to forge a bond of confidence and respect between them. Teamwork between them was a must. A good engine-crew worked by their experience of each other and an almost telepathic communication could develop.

I have already mentioned some of the tasks the fireman had to do in addition to actually firing the engine. His main duties were to check the water in the boiler and to shovel coal into the firebox. But it was not quite as simple as that, and this is where teamwork and a knowledge of the road was essential.

The fireman had to know if they were coming to a stiff climb so that he could build up a strong fire and fill up the boiler in advance. The driver would then have a good head of steam. The fireman had to be alert all the time so as to anticipate the changing demands upon the engine throughout the journey; it required intelligence and a good deal of experience to make the boiler produce just the amount of steam needed at any one time. Running the water level down too far and having to put the injectors on at the wrong time would make the steam pressure drop by an appreciable amount. On the other hand, stoking up the fire when there was little demand for steam, when descending a bank for instance, allowed too much steam to escape wastefully from the safety-valves. It was reckoned that on an average size locomotive, some ten pounds of coal was wasted for every minute that the safety-valves were open.

Coming on duty, generally before the driver, the fireman was responsible for checking the engine over. He had to inspect the water level in the boiler; examine the fire to ensure that it was clean and not choked with clinker; check for leaks in the tube-plates and tubes; ensure that the sand-boxes were full and working, and that the head-lamps were all present, filled and trimmed, also a complete set of disc boards, and fire irons.

When the driver came on duty the fireman had to assist him in checking the locomotive and in oiling round. The last two jobs before leaving the shed were to fill up with water and to examine the coal-bunker or tender.

It was this preparation of the locomotive, and especially its disposal at the end of the day, when booking off duty, that the enginemen disliked most. Once inside the shed limits there are no signals, and in foggy weather – not uncommon in the East End of London in those days – after disposal, it was every man for himself and devil take the hindmost! Everybody wanted to get home, and the best man won.

The time allowed for preparation was 45 minutes for tank engines and one hour for tenders from the time of booking on duty to taking the engine out of the shed. Fifteen minutes of this time was taken up in signing on, reading the notices, finding out what road of the shed your engine was on or, indeed, if it had arrived back at the shed. At such a big shed as Stratford in particular it was no easy matter to locate your allotted engine.

The fireman first went to the stores to collect the necessary equipment for the diagram booked to him. This would include four types of oils; for engine, cylinders, paraffin for the headlamps and rape oil for the gauge glass lamps. In addition, there was 'Paragon' grease for the Westinghouse brake pump.

Before World War I a ball of tallow was also issued. This was melted on the oil tray over the firehole in the cab, and mixed with the cylinder oil. Tallow ceased to be issued soon after War broke out, reputedly because it came from Russia and was difficult to obtain. It was also issued to cleaners, as it could be applied to the smokebox to give it a new look, or smeared on the blue paintwork to give it a sheen, or produce wavy patterns.

The storeman also issued keys to the toolboxes on the engine, and the headlamps; four of them. If the driver had now arrived he would help the fireman carry all this gear to the engine.

On reaching it, the fun would start. If there was enough steam pressure, and enough room between your engine and the others on the same road, it could be set up for oiling. Space in which to move was important. Certain mechanical parts were impossible to get at, such as side rods which became inaccessible on some classes if they were up under the side-valancing. Each had its own recognised positions for oiling, some having to be set twice. Whilst the fireman was oiling up, the driver would have other work to attend to, checking the brake and so on.

The previous driver to have run the engine would leave a list of any defects and points for attention for the last man to book. This list would be placed in a clip on the footplate.

After filling up the tank with water, the crew could generally relax, but not so at large sheds, particularly Stratford, and especially so with a tender engine. In this instance the driver would have to consider whether to turn his charge, and by which exit to leave the shed to arrive on his booked train the right way round. This was also an important point when taking out a shunting engine, to ensure that the driver was on the correct side of the footplate for the best view of the shunter.

The bulk of the work in disposing an engine fell squarely on the fireman's shoulders. The work started when the engine was positioned over the ash-pit, and again different times were allowed for disposal according to the class. For a tank engine it was one hour. Forty-five minutes were allotted for the driver to examine the engine and book any faults, reporting the most important to the foreman and perhaps the boilermaker or fitter if applicable.

On occasion the driver might require the fireman to position the engine to check for 'blows', that is defects in the valves or pistons that allowed steam to pass abnormally. This is where a detailed knowledge of the workings of the valves and cylinders was essential. It would be necessary to position the loco so that the pistons and valves were in certain positions: then by opening and shutting the regulator with the brakes on, and altering the position of the reversing gear, any defects in valves or pistons would become apparent – by noting whether or not a puff of steam was released from the chimney. Depending on how the engine was set, the driver could ascertain which piston or valve was defective, and even which part of a valve needed attention.

Generally the fireman had enough to do with his own allotted tasks. This included cleaning the fire, or throwing it out if the engine was booked for shed, raking out the ashpan, and cleaning the ashes from the smokebox. The latter was always an unpleasant task, the more so if the wind was in the wrong direction, making the job quite intolerable.

The remaining fifteen minutes were allowed for having the engine coaled up, returning the oil bottles, lamps and keys to the stores, and lastly putting the engine into the position in the shed as required.

Filling up with coal was done when the engine came on shed and it was a favourite dodge for the coalman to throw a large lump into the bottom of the bunker to avoid having to break it up, and then cover it with smaller lumps. This made their job lighter, as the bunker soon appeared to be full. The large lump would form a bridge and stop the rest of the coal coming through the coal door at the front of the tender. Freeing such an obstruction could be very tricky for a fireman once on the move.

An hour was also allocated for disposal of a tender engine, but this time was apportioned differently. The full hour was allowed for the examination and cleaning the fire, and it was left for men booked for 'Preparation and Disposal' (or P & D as it was known) to put the engine away.

On his first trip out, the footplate novice soon finds that trying to shovel coal into a two foot-diameter hole whilst an engine is moving is a lot different from doing it when stationary. The passenger sitting back in the train has no idea of the rough buffeting the crew up front are getting. Locomotives are provided with stiff springs, since too much vertical movement of the axles in their guides plays havoc with the 'valve events' taking place in the cylinders. The design of valve gear depends on there being very little relative movement between the driving axle and the centre-line of the cylinders.

When the regulator is opened from a dead start, especially with a heavy train and a greasy rail, real experience is needed to prevent the wheels from slipping and the resulting blast from tearing the fire to pieces. For the first revolution, the reversing lever should not be touched, the regulator being opened gently until the engine gets a start, but even then 'notching-up' should not be hurried. If the reversing lever position is altered, the engine tends to impart an obvious fore- and -aft motion which can sometimes be felt in the first carriage of the train – a sensation rather like that of riding a bicycle across a ploughed field!

Like all novice firemen, on my first trip, I put more coal on the floor than through the firehole; this would be there in front of you one instant, only to move in the next, so that your shovel would

The original G. E. R. Claud Hamilton, No.1900, in original condition   Overleaf: The footplate of Claud Hamilton showing the apparatus for oil-burning and the original type of air-reversing gear on the right-hand side.

[L. D. Brooks Collection]

strike the side, depositing coal all over the floorboards. However, after the first day or so, the skill of aiming one's shovel through the hole is acquired. This then allows a fireman to concentrate more on dropping the coal onto the right place in the firebox.

The golden rule of firing was 'little and often', spreading four or five shovelfuls over the grate at frequent intervals, depending on the work being done by the engine. It was a matter of experience to know the depth of fire that worked best for the particular locomotive class and for the job to be done. But it was most important to keep the firebed depth even all over, always tending to keep the fire slightly thicker round the walls of the fire box than in the middle. Thick patches of coal would result in cool spots and the steam pressure would fall. Thick patches would also cause incomplete combustion of the coal, resulting in black smoke. On the other hand, a thin patch in the fire could be just as bad: this would allow cold air to be drawn through the grate, again causing a fall in pressure.

The fire had to be cleaned periodically with the pricker, the grandfather of the household poker. Six or more feet long, it consisted of a steel rod, with a loop at one end to hold on to. This, as the name implies, was used to prick the firebed to break up the clinker, which on a long trip would build up and restrict the passage of air through the firebed, thus inhibiting the steaming capacity of the boiler and resulting in thick black smoke.

Observing the smoke from the chimney was a good indicator to the fireman of conditions in the firebox. Black smoke indicated that for various reasons not enough air was getting through. No smoke meant that too much air was getting through, so it was best to fire to a happy medium. Best results were when the chimney produced light grey smoke.

The fireman had to control the air-flow to the fire by opening the firehole door. On Great Eastern engines, the doors were fitted with a ratchet device to enable them to be set in several positions and this did much to aid combustion.

Additionally, there were 'dampers' or doors fitted to the ashpan, which were operated from the cab. These could also be opened or closed on a ratchet to regulate the amount of air through the firebed, although generally they were always open.

Of course, the air-flow through the fire was produced by the action of exhausted steam from the cylinders passing through the blast pipe, causing a vacuum in the smokebox. When the regulator was closed, vacuum was maintained by the blower producing the same effect. The driver had to open the blower before closing the regulator and conversely open the regulator before shutting the blower. The consequences of not doing so could be, and sometimes were, fatal. If the smokebox vacuum were to be interrupted, the flow of air to the fire would be stopped with unfortunate results. Combustion can only occur where there is air available, with the implication that the fire could leap out of the firehole into the cab, to obtain oxygen. It was therefore always advisable to use the blower when firing.

This phenomenon, known as a 'blowback', could also be caused by tunnels or low bridges interrupting the air-flow to the ashpan. For this reason, a driver had to remember to open the blower fully also on approaching these.

The fireman had to arrange his firing to suit the journey in order to be able to look out for signals that were more easily visible from his side of the footplate. I remember on one occasion when I was firing to the miserable old so-and-so who was my first driver, I looked out of the cab for a particular signal and called out to him, "Off!" – the railwayman's term for a signal showing 'clear to proceed'. However, he immediately shut the regulator and applied the brakes before realising that the signal was off. He then blamed me for saying that it was on. I explained what I had said, but he replied, "A signal is either 'off' or 'on' so try to speak plain."

I fired to this particular driver for two years and at least he taught me how *not* to drive an engine. His grumpiness could be attributed to ill-health, but he had no judgment in stopping a train, or in getting the best out of an engine by using what is termed expansive working.

All drivers had their own ideas how best to work an engine. In driving 'on the regulator', full-gear was used to get the train away and once on the move the reverser was brought back to about 30 per cent cut-off, the rest of the driving being done by moving the regulator to a quarter, half, three-quarters or fully open as conditions required. This method was very wasteful on steam, and consequently on coal – not to mention hard on the fireman's back!

In the other method – expansive working – advantage was taken of the fact that after the steam supply to the cylinder had been cut off it continued to expand and push the piston to the end of its stroke. This resulted in economies all round; the regulator could be left half or a quarter open for most of the journey, with the speed controlled by increasing or decreasing the cut-off of the valve-gear. Steam taken from the boiler was reduced to the minimum, burning less coal. The exhaust pressure was much lower because the steam was expanded a great deal before the exhaust port was opened. This meant that the engine was free running since it did not have to push large quantities of high-pressure steam out of the blast-pipe.

If you have never driven a steam engine, this technical description of how to go about it may, of course, be difficult to understand. In later years, the tip I used to give firemen who came to our improvement class for passing out as driver was simple – "When the time comes to use the reversing lever or wheel, to shorten the stroke of the valves, never quite lose the sound of the beats from the chimney. If you do, you've got it wrong."

My next driver that I worked with knew the art of expansive working very well and for the first day or two with him I was quite unprepared for the easy and gentle way that he worked the engine. In fact, I wasted more steam by blowing off than he used in moving the train.

At this time the G.E.R. was providing the most intensive steam-operated suburban services in the world, namely the 'Jazz service'. This required strict timekeeping; our timetable showed things to the nearest half-a-minute and we had to keep to them. A minute late at a junction could delay a train on another line, or mean that we were held up and missed our path in the timetable. It may therefore seem strange that no 'Buck', 'Gobbler' or 'Claud' – in fact no engine of any type on which I had been firing or driving up to this time – was equipped with a speedometer. Moreover, no watch was ever supplied by the Company!

A good deal of the suburban work was done by the 'Buckjumpers' or 'Bucks' – small 0–6–0 tanks with 4' diameter wheels. Seeing one at the head of a ten-coach suburban train might lead one to think this engine incapable of moving it, but it did, and very well too!

They got their nickname from the rapid way they started into motion: having small wheels, speed was quickly attained, enabling the engine to coast along thereafter. Then at a station the brake would be sharply applied, bringing the train equally smartly to a halt. The brake used on the G.E.R. was the Westinghouse compressed-air brake which was reliable, quick-acting and allowed very good precision in its operation. At the next station, the regulator would be opened fully and the little engine would get away again very smartly, with good acceleration. This rapid starting and stopping, plus the bucking and jumping motion on the footplate, gave rise to their nickname.

Bill, my new driver, had a driving tip which I never forgot. "A 'Buck' will never increase steam pressure with the regulator open, but only when coasting," he used to say. With sixteen stops on the Enfield line, this maxim stood me in good stead in later years, whilst stopping the train exactly at the platform, at every station, with the Westinghouse brake, was an education in itself.

Bill was one of the calmest drivers that I ever knew. I recollect our booking on together one Sunday morning at Enfield shed. As usual, he left me to do the oiling whilst he did the fireman's work to get his fat down. It was regular practice (although against the rules) that when there was a good supply of fuel available at the coal stage the fireman, assisted by the driver, would fill the firebox to the limit. Bill remarked at the time, "That little lot will take your nearly all the way to Liverpool Street and back without touching the shovel!" We started away from Enfield with a full train and everything in apple-pie order, but I could not help feeling uneasy about something. As we approached Edmonton, the penny dropped. "Bill," I said, "I forgot to fill up the tank at Enfield."

As we ground to a halt at the platform, I leapt out of the cab and scrambled up on top of the tank to look down the filler hole. The tank filler cap on a 'Buck' was about a foot in diameter and opened into a deep cylindrical sieve that reached almost to the bottom of the tank. There was no water to be seen, which meant that we had no more than a few inches in there at the best.

The coal banked up in the firebox under the door hadn't even ignited yet and with the dampers shut I managed to ease out two great lumps of coal with my bare hands. As a consequence of my oversight the driver was now faced with a decision; either to fail the engine and return to Enfield, landing us both in the cart, or to carry on to London and take water when we arrived, there being no water-crane available to us in between.

Bill decided on the latter course of action, but not without emphasising that he would decide when, and for how long, the injectors were to be used; also how the dampers were to be operated so as to prevent blowing-off, thereby conserving water.

Off we went, with Bill quite relaxed and confident. At length, we arrived at Liverpool Street on time, and believe me I heaved a heavy sigh of relief when we finally stopped at the water crane!

CHAPTER FIVE

Moving into the Upper Class: 1921

In 1921 I left Enfield and transferred to the parent depot, Stratford, to maintain my seniority in line for promotion. This transfer took place in Easter week and my first duties were on excursion trains to Southend with another miserable old so-and-so of a driver. I remember our engine was one of the later Y14 goods type that had been fitted with Westinghouse brakes for just this type of work. I don't know whether it was me, but it made a poor job of climbing Brentwood and Billericay banks, and driver Wiseman did not help matters. Wheels of 4′11″ diameter do not make for high speeds, and the greater number of revolutions needed to cover a set distance, compared with the larger 'drivers' of a passenger engine, soon ate up all the steam that the boiler could produce.

However, I was soon put in my proper link with a fine driver, Fred Reeves. This was a long-distance goods with a regular engine, one of the 'Little Goods', No.828. It was one of the early members of the class, built in 1887 at Stratford works, but thirty-four years and a couple of new boilers later, she was still in fine fettle. Indeed, she was not scrapped until the end of 1949.

The engines on the Great Eastern at this time were a drab sight. The Admiralty had commandeered all stocks of paint at the outbreak of War in 1914 and from then on all locomotives, when repainted or built new, were left in the grey undercoat in anticipation of repainting in the former glossy blue or black upon the cessation of hostilities.

The end of the War came but none of the engines were, in fact, repainted in their former glory. True, a handful of them came through this period without a repaint, but the blue engines were few and far between. Shortage of manpower meant that the engines were generally dirty, although the grey livery could look quite nice when new, relieved by the red-painted buffer beams, side-rods and number plates. The engine number was repeated on the tender or tank sides in large yellow figures which was done when the 'train control' system was introduced in 1921.

I remained in this link with 828 for the next two years. She was a splendid engine and I soon got used to her likes and dislikes. She wouldn't steam freely with a thick fire but with firing little and often she responded well to the shovel. It was one of those quirks that gave a locomotive personality: two essentially identical ones had to be handled in different ways and it was a matter of getting used to them. A case in point was our famous express No. 1900 *Claud Hamilton* and her sisters. As a whole they were excellent machines, but somehow No. 1900 herself was poor by comparison, even after extensive rebuilding in the 1930s.

Our regular job was night work on goods trains, taking our rest mostly at Yarmouth, Norwich, Kings Lynn and so on. This meant finishing our turn of duty at one of these depots and then, after resting, booking on duty for the return trip home. On arrival at the destination depot we would be told where to lodge, and if the landlady already had too many lodgers we had to wait our turn before going to bed. Many a time the bed would still be warm!

It was about then that I began to take an interest in Union work, as upon joining the Stratford branch of A.S.L.E.F., Bill Stevenson, who was Branch Secretary at the time, found out that I should have had my wages adjusted to the same as that of the junior man at Stratford, and not that of the Enfield junior. This meant that I received nearly £10 in back pay – then a considerable sum of money.

My next firing link was on the vacuum-connected goods trains to Whitemoor and back each night. This move coincided with the Grouping in 1923 under which the Great Eastern became part of the London & North Eastern Railway along with the Great Northern, Great Central, North Eastern, North British and Great North of Scotland Railways.

The new administration lost no time in moving engines about and in my new link we acquired one from the Great Northern, No. 1639, one of the large outside-cylinder 2-6-0s, and still painted green. This was a stranger to us on the G.E. as it had no steam brake, and the vacuum instead of the Westinghouse compressed air brake for

The famous 0–10–0WT built to prove that steam power could accelerate a loaded passenger train as fast as electric power. Built in 1902, she was known as the 'Decapod', and was later rebuilt as an 0–8–0 tender engine.
[W. O. Skeat Collection]

the train. However, my experience working in the R.O.D. on various British and foreign engines stood me in good stead. Firing through a trap in the firehole door was not strange to me, but the coal had to be broken up small to get it into the firebox.

We worked this 2–6–0 for nearly a month, when one night an ex-G.N.R. Inspector appeared and informed us that he would be riding with us to show us how to work it. On the night in question, in fact, we had a different engine of the same class, but this one was very dull for steam. We set off as usual, and after stopping for water at Whittlesford, with the next stop Whitemoor, the Inspector picked up the shovel in order to show me how it *should* be done. Glad of a rest from my efforts, I stood back and left him to it. I was still somewhat annoyed by one of his cracks before he had taken over at Whittlesford. "Fireman", he had said, "always use your brain to save your arms". However, it very soon became apparent that our 'expert' was having no luck either, getting hot under the collar and more steamed up than the engine!

I settled myself down to gloat, observing that my driver wasn't helping the poor chap much by easing the regulator as a more sympathetic one might have done! All in all, we must have burnt a good five tons of coal that night. It's a pity that our friend didn't show us how it should have been done with a good engine. This one, we later found out, had three superheater elements blowing!

I enjoyed being in this link. Perhaps it was the challenge of having a strange engine to master. Or it could have been the three shifts on nights with one day shift on the Epping Goods: 'convalescent', as it was called. This gave the engineman a chance to clean up, pack glands on leaky steam cocks in the cab, change faulty gauge glasses and do umpteen other little jobs to make the night shift easier.

Following this link, I moved up on to the 'long-legged' engines, that is those with big driving wheels on the passenger runs: the 'Claud' 4–4–0s, the 1500 4–6–0s and the new 1800 class B17 'Sandringham' three-cylinder 4–6–0. By this time, the initial upheaval of the Grouping was over and engines were being repainted in their new L.N.E.R. colours: apple green for express engines, lined in black and white, and black for the rest, the passenger engines being additionally lined-out. All engines now carried the initials of their new owners on the tank or tender sides in shaded gold or yellow letters, together with their new numbers. On the G.E. section, engines had been renumbered by adding 7000 to their old numbers;

thus our 'Gobbler' with the magic number 1 had now become the rather insignificant number 7001. Our large 4–6–0s were now the '8500s', but they always remained '1500s' to us!

My new link was a very large one and took about six months to work full-cycle. We had practically no regular engine because the work was spaced out with spells on 'odd duty', deputising for sickness, or on 'specials', and long-distance stopping passenger trains.

When on 'odd duty' the driver and his mate were often parted, perhaps the driver covering for sickness and the fireman filling in on any firing position as necessary. Through all of these links, a fireman was of course learning the road, gradients, signals, etc., and all about the various engine classes; how best to drive and fire them, and of course their particular methods of preparation and disposal.

Within a year I had moved up into the 'scoop' link, always with a regular engine and regular driver. This involved working non-stop expresses between Liverpool Street and Yarmouth, Cromer and Lowestoft, which meant replenishing the water tanks in the tender from water troughs – hence the name. There were two sets at this time on the G.E. section: one at Halifax Junction on the London side of Ipswich, and the other at Tivetshall, between Diss and Norwich.

The troughs were adjacent to one another between each pair of running tracks, and on our engines the driver was on the right-hand side of the footplate, so that he had to call out to the fireman when to raise and lower the scoop.

Originally, G.E. express locos had water scoops operated by compressed-air. A small brass handle was located behind the hand-brake column at the front of the tender. This was locked with a small padlock so that the scoop could not be dropped inadvertently.

The speed of the train was important when scooping: too slow meant that there was insufficient force to fill up the tender, whereas travelling too fast resulted in picking up more air than water. One only found this out after one had lifted the scoop and the water gauge had settled down! Remember, engines in those days had no speedometers, and one's velocity had to be judged solely from experience, which was especially difficult in the dark.

A trip on the 'Yarmouth Scoop' started at Stratford an hour and a half before the booked departure time, this period being occupied in preparing the engine and taking it up to Liverpool Street, generally with empty stock. Our regular engine was 1500 class No. 8559.

Preparation was carried out in the usual fashion, the fireman checking the sand, fixing the smokebox door securely in place, checking the fire and making sure of a complete set of lamps and headcode discs. Also ensuring that there was enough water in the tender.

If he thought the tender would take another half-ton of coal, he would draw the driver's attention to it. This would save having to reach so far back into the tender during the trip. The driver meanwhile was checking the notices and repair book, testing the brakes, gauges and scoop, also oiling up. On an engine with a mechanical lubricator, this entailed giving the operating wheel a couple of turns to ensure that the feed pipes to the cylinders were filled with oil.

When leaving the shed for the trip to Liverpool Street it was a favourite trick to be one of several engines travelling to London together, and not to open the regulator but let the other engines do the work. This gave me a chance to work my way round the engine and open the smokebox door and pour some thick oil down the blast-pipe. This found its way into the valves and made the reverser easier to work. Of course, we had to continue for a bit without opening the regulator during the trip, to allow the oil to do its job – otherwise it would be ejected from the chimney and smother everything around.

Upon arrival at Liverpool Street, we would back onto the train and it was my job to couple up. Even today, Liverpool Street station is one of the few places on British Railways where coupling and uncoupling is performed by the fireman (or secondman as he is known today), instead of by a shunter.

The coupling procedure was always carried out in the same order: firstly the steam heating hoses were connected, as they were the lowest; then the coupling, screwing it up tight, according to the book. Sometimes, if the driver was watching, he might instruct the fireman to loosen it a turn or so to allow a little slack for starting away. Lastly the brake hoses would be connected.

Brakes were a complicated subject on the Great Eastern line. Before the grouping, all of our passenger trains had just the Westinghouse brake, but the fitted goods stock had the vacuum brake. This was in common with the other railways, as goods stock could work all over Britain. Accordingly, a few G.E. engines had both Westinghouse and vacuum brakes.

With the Grouping, most of those which formed the L.N.E.R. used the vacuum brake and it therefore became standard. The 'Westinghouse lines' such as the G.E.R. and the North Eastern were duly converted. However, in the early 1920s an attempt was made to convert the suburban services also to vacuum brake, but it was found that its slower operation, both on application and release, made it difficult to keep time. Thus the suburban services retained Westinghouse brakes whilst the other services went over to vacuum. The result was that all our Westinghouse-fitted engines were in fact dual-fitted by the L.N.E.R. The general increase of fitted goods trains meant that many of the other engines which previously had no train brakes were given the vacuum brake. Coaching stock for the express services and non-suburban trains was also converted but, as this could not be accomplished overnight, there was some overlap: much of the coaching stock thus had one type of brake with a through pipe in readiness for the other. Therefore when coupling up to a train, one was frequently faced with both vacuum and Westinghouse pipes. Both were coupled up. We soon found out which was operative on the train when carrying out the statutory brake test before departure.

CHAPTER SIX

The 12.30pm from Liverpool Street to Yarmouth

IN THE FIVE to ten minutes before departure, the driver would give the engine a final oil-round, wash his hands and check that the gauges were all registering satisfactorily.

When the starting signal went off we looked for the right-away from the guard if he was at the front of the train, or from the station foreman if the guard was at the back. When this was given, the driver would open the regulator slightly, although not too much or the engine would slip its wheels. This was where slackening the coupling played its part: with large-wheeled engines especially, much depended on the first exhaust beat, and a slack coupling gave just that extra room for the initial movement before taking the weight of the train. When starting, the exhaust beats seem a long time in between. For a two-cylinder 1500, with 6'6" wheels, the engine had in fact to travel nearly six feet between exhaust beats.

Meantime, I would be having a last look back down the train to check for any open doors or for any signal from the guard to stop.

No coal would have been put on the fire for some time; it was essential to build this up before leaving so that the coal was burning through at departure time. Similary the boiler would have been filled up. Putting fresh coal on when starting away, or just before, cooled the fire just when it needed to be at its hottest. Putting the injector on at this time would also be detrimental to the engine's starting power.

Departure time on this train was 12.30pm due at Yarmouth at 3.0pm; a two-and-a-half hour run in front of us.

Express passenger, suburban and goods trains were all different in the way they were worked, quite apart from their speed. On an express, the fireman knew that once the regulator was open, it virtually remained so. Once under way, the driver would drive on the reverser, shortening and lengthening the cut-off of the valves to suit the speed and conditions. Shortening the stroke too much caused back-pressure in the cylinders and impeded the free-running of the engine. Lengthening its travel likewise caused back-pressure, in that the momentum of the engine is wasted in pushing large quantities of steam out of the cylinders, the resultant blasts of the exhaust ripping the fire to shreds. This burned the coal too fast and produced more steam than the engine could gainfully employ.

Much depended upon the driver's experience and thus if the fireman was equal to his job, the responsibility for maintaining steam and using the coal and water economically rested on the driver as much as the fireman.

Almost immediately after leaving Liverpool Street and traversing the curves outside the station the train is at the foot of the 1 in 70 Bethnal Green bank. An engine really has to dig its heels in here, and half-way up I would put the exhaust steam injector on, regulating the water feed to the boiler to as low as possible, until I could see from the gauge how the engine was steaming. Too much water in the boiler could affect the performance of the superheater, and in the possibility that the driver may have to shut the regulator, I had to allow room to turn the injector full on to stop the engine blowing off.

Up to Stratford our speed was never much different from that of an ordinary passenger train, owing to the various permanent speed orders – which have been eased slightly in recent years.

I would gradually build up the thickness of the fire, adding a few shovelfuls at a time around the box knowing that after passing Maryland the engine would be getting a move-on. All being well, each distant signal would be off, and the driver would open the regulator fully and at the same time ensure that the reversing wheel was fully locked. For the fireman it was practically continuous work – adding little and often all over the box.

No.8559 would be steadily gaining momentum as we stormed through Ilford, and as our speed increased the driver would progressively shorten the valve-travel. Approaching Romford, I would be concentrating carefully on building up the fire in readiness for Brentwood bank, using the shovel as a shade against the glare, seeing where the fire was burning thin.

The most famous of the 'Little Goods' 0–6–0 tender engines, No.930, which was built in record time at Stratford Works in 1891.
[L. D. Brooks Collection]

The footplate of one of the later 'Little Goods' 0–6–0s, fitted with both Westinghouse and vacuum brakes. Known on the G.E.R. as the Y14 class, and later the L.N.E.R. J15 class, several survived until the elimination of steam from the G.E. section in 1962.
[L.C.G.B.: Ken Nunn Coll

This is another example of how road knowledge was essential as much for the fireman as for the driver. The addition of more coal would mean that the steam-pressure would be hovering around the 175lbs mark by the time we reached the bank, but the driver would lengthen the cut-off, and as the increased draught took effect, and with me adding small shovelfuls of coal as we climbed the bank, the gauge needle would come up to 180.

The driver might check his watch, knowing the time we were booked to pass Shenfield, and would give me the thumbs-up. Upon approaching the Southend junction, he would ease the regulator. Slightly down-hill now and with the work behind us for a while, we would both have a mug of tea; I would open my food bag, ignoring the coal dust, and occasionally peering in the firebox, adding the odd shovelful as necessary.

Due to a permanent speed order at Chelmsford, the regulator would be closed and the brake applied slightly to check our speed, whilst I was busy re-building the fire ready for acceleration again, plus adjusting the injector to prevent blowing-off. Then after Chelmsford it was full speed to Colchester; as a fireman once re-marked when passing Witham, "My word, mate, she's really laying her ears back now!"

There was another permanent speed order at Colchester, owing to the curves through the station. It was always a temptation to over-step the mark here to get a good run up to Parson's Heath.

Approaching Manningtree, the distant signal was visible high over the trees and if it was off it would save me from using the shovel before the rise to the other side. Once through Bentley it was time to see about using the scoop at Halifax Junction. Up to this point I would still be feeding the fire, and just before scooping I would shut off the injectors. They would fail if I did not, as the action of scoop-ing caused air bubbles in the tender. As already described, getting the engine's speed right at the moment of scooping was important to picking up water efficiently.

Again we had to slow down for Ipswich tunnel, and I had to be careful to adjust the damper doors to avoid blow-back. Passing Ipswich station and the speed restriction there, we take the Yar-mouth road and so on the Westerfield. Next came the difficult bit, loathed and cursed by all G.E. enginemen as the line drops down to Woodbridge which is at the bottom of a dip. To crown it all there was a 10mph speed restriction here due, I was told, to the boggy condition of the land. Engines at this time had no speed indicators, as already mentioned, and the 10mph had to be judged by the driver. The temptation was to over-estimate, in order to get a good crack at the bank on the other side.

I was concerned that we did not slow too much because of the additional steam required to get up the other side: the fire at this stage would be in poor condition due to the 'slack' at Ipswich causing the formation of clinker. However, with the fire-hole door put up a couple of notches, 8559 would usually climb the bank, and all would be plain sailing except for the two wooden swing bridges at St. Olaves and Reedham. Each of these was restricted to 4m.p.h., and to enforce this we had to pick up pilotmen before crossing. They, of course, tended to err on the side of safety. Consequently each bridge took about five minutes to cross.

During this time, the pilotmen would take orders for rabbits, which we could collect on our return journey! I well remember the price of these was 6d each initially, but inflation was rife even in those days, and although the price of each rabbit at each bridge was the same, the prices gradually crept up to 9d and later to the old one shilling. Some of our mates for whom we took orders swore that we were in the rabbit business ourselves!

Before we parted company, we would leave a deposit of a couple of new sponge cloths and the promise of a lump or two of coal on the return journey. It would be my job to scratch about in the tender for a couple of respectable lumps, as we were scraping the barrel by this time.

From the bridges to Yarmouth the main part of the work was over for the driver, but it was a bit of a struggle for me. The stopping and starting usually caused the fire to die down somewhat, the steam pressure to drop and clinker would be choking the firebars. The pricker did not seem to help a great deal, and with the firedoor practically shut, we generally would run into Yarmouth with a half a glass of water and the pressure down to 170 or even 160 lbs.

Fortunately, we had a relief crew who took the engine and prepared it for our return journey, while we attended to the inner man.

The advent of the three-cylinder B17 class 'Sandringhams' from 1928 displaced the 1500s and 'Super Claud' 4–4–0s from the heavier expresses. Amongst other destinations, some were sent to Southend shed. Here, the men kept the cabs as clean as was possible, with all of the brass-work shining – a contrast to the exteriors of the engines, where the only cleaning done was a rectangular patch around the number. All the locomotives of the Great Eastern, especially the expresses at this time, were worked to death. Parts for maintenance were hard to get, so the Company had its work cut out to give the men their regular engines, which was always done if possible.

This brings me to an incident that occurred whilst I was on the 'Yarmouth scoop' roster. Coming on duty, I noticed that our usual 1500, No.8559, was missing from the list. I enquired of the foreman as to which engine to prepare and he told me 7555, saying that this was the only one available.

No.7555 was a Y14 Little Goods, equipped with passenger brakes, but no water scoop. To make matters worse, my regular mate did not turn up for duty. Meanwhile, I got on with preparing the engine, then one of the spare drivers arrived on the footplate, and his first words were, "What's the job, Jim?"

"Yarmouth scoop," says I.

His jaw dropped. "What! With this?" he exclaimed and, seeing that I was serious, stormed off to the foreman's office.

The outcome was that the foreman asked Liverpool Street if they could arrange an exchange. We took our 0–6–0 up to London and backed on to the train, then waited . . . Time ticked by and with each passing minute it looked more and more likely that our ancient-looking engine, with its long chimney and low boiler, would be steaming bravely out of Liverpool Street with little hope of getting very far!

However, we were saved by the arrival alongside of 'Super Claud' No.8788 with a Southend crew aboard who had instructions to change engines. The 4–4–0 was as clean as a new pin, inside and out, with a huge DeWrance sight-feed lubricator filling the fireman's seat. My first job was to check the operation of the water scoop and I asked the Southend fireman for the key to unlock it.

Having done no more arduous duties in recent months than working Liverpool Street to Southend trains it was not surprising that the fireman replied with a grin that the key was missing. The smile disappeared from his face when I 'unlocked' the padlock with the coal-hammer! I found that with a bit of nursing the scoop worked enough for us to use.

And so we were away to Yarmouth, somewhat apprehensive whether 8788 would do the job without a lot of persuasion. However, we had no cause for worry. She kept time easily and laid her ears down just as well as 8559. It was my first experience of a 'Claud' on a long run, and I was impressed. She steamed beautifully and rode very smoothly.

One incident I must mention, whilst in this link, as it illustrates very well the practicality of small driving wheels for a suburban engine and large wheels for an express engine. One of our jobs was working the 5.39pm Liverpool Street to Southend, non-stop to Billericay, with a 1500 4–6–0 with 6'6" wheels. At the same time as we started, a Gidea Park train departed, non-stop to Romford, behind one of the later L.N.E.R.-built N7 0–6–2 tanks which had 4'10" drivers. He forged ahead in grand style; we saw him passing Bethnal Green as we rounded the curve at the bottom of the bank, and again we sighted him at Forest Gate as we came into the straight at Maryland Point. But we caught up with him at Manor Park and had overtaken him by Ilford, a graphic illustration, I thought, of how small wheels were better for acceleration, but large wheels were essential for continous speed. A 1500, for example, would have been a washout on the 'Jazz'.

The word 'Jazz' became part of our lingo when the suburban service was greatly improved in 1920. There were more trains and a quicker service both in the timing and number of trains per hour. As a result, various trains called at some stations but not others and this improved running between the termini. Another feature which was to occur at the same time was the colouring of the various carriages, denoting whether they were third, second, or first class. A broad band of paint of appropriate colour was added to the long panel just beneath the roofing; yellow was for third class, blue for second and first was left alone – hence the nickname from these jazzy colours.

Working down to Ipswich in the summer was always a pleasant experience. One summer's afternoon we had worked down with an express and were booked on a parcels train back to London, stopping at intermediate stations. We halted at Shenfield on the way back and while we were waiting for the unloading and loading to be completed, my mate started looking around the cab floor and asking me if I saw something. But my eyes were on the platform awaiting the right away.

"I saw either a leaf or a mouse on the floor!" he said.

At that moment we were given the signal, being booked to shunt into the now-removed siding at Ingrave, just before Brentwood. This done, we set about clearing up the mystery. I gave the footplate a good sweeping and, having a few crumbs left from our 'iron rations', we sprinkled these around the floor and waited like a couple of tom cats.

Sure enough, a mouse came out from under the floor-boards near the boiler and helped himself to the crumbs. Then the train that we had been shunted clear of screamed past and he flew back from whence he came. How he got there is anybody's guess. It must have been a tedious climb for a mouse, from rail-level to the footplate! This was the only mouse I ever saw on a footplate, but engines certainly did get fleas. The men in the boiler-shops at Stratford used to hate stripping the asbestos lagging from certain locos as this was home to thousands of parasites. Again it is a mystery how they got there, or even how they managed to survive the high temperatures.

Before leaving my firing career it would be wrong not to set on record details of my worst trip ever, which at the same time was quite an extraordinary one.

It was 1924, at the time of the Wembley Exhibition, and the old Great Central Section enquired of Stratford whether they could supply an engine, crew, and rolling stock for an excursion from Derby to Wembley for the staff of the Rolls-Royce Company. Unaware of these goings-on 'higher-up' I put in for the Saturday off, as I wished to travel to Derby to make arrangements for my wedding, which was to take place later that year. I was blankly refused time off by the foreman, who added, "You won't even be at Stratford that Friday and Saturday. You and your driver are booked for the Derby job." I was in clover; I could visit my old pal Syd in Derby – who was to be best man at the wedding – *and* get paid for it!

The job consisted of working empty carriages from Temple Mills to Derby, on the Friday, and the following day working the excursion from there to Wembley, stabling the engine at Neasden.

The engine we had was 8532, the fitters having been working on her all the previous day. We were also told not to use the water scoop on the Great Central section as the troughs were of a different size, but this information did not concern us much, as this was the G.C. pilotman's headache. We worked the train as far as we knew the road, that is to Whitemoor, then picked up the pilotman and put him in the picture regarding the water scoop. He asked me if my fire needed cleaning, as we had another 100 miles to go. It was in good condition and I decided to take my chances; cleaning a fire in a hot summer's day isn't anyone's cup of tea, least of all mine!

We arrived at Derby Friargate around 4pm and disposed of the engine ourselves. As we booked off, we were told to present ourselves at one o'clock next morning, to work the train back to

Wembley at 3am. After this we were shown our lodgings. Some lodge! There were half-a-dozen nippers sitting at table, and the cleanliness was conspicuous by absence!

However, in the evening I took the train to Darley Dale where my pal lived, made my arrangements, and then returned to our 'hotel'. There were four single beds in the room; two were occupied by another driver and fireman, and one by my driver. All were asleep by then, each giving a good impression of a weary expert sawing wood, so my rest was, to say the least, disturbed.

At about half-past midnight we were wakened for the return journey. I had previously been lodging with my cousin at Leyton and she had packed me some eggs and bacon to fry. But when I found the frying pan, I decided I'd sooner eat them raw with plain bread. Fortunately we had brought our own tea and sugar; one big brew filled each of our bottles.

When we arrived at the shed we were treated like VIPs: fitters and cleaners were in attendance, one of the latter showing us the oil stores so that we could draw all the necessaries.

Fastened to the front of the smokebox door, and of about the same diameter, was a circular board bearing the words 'Rolls-Royce Excursion to Wembley 1924'. I wish now that I had examined this board more carefully or I might have discovered that the smokebox door wasn't properly tightened.

Our route to Wembley, so the pilotman informed us, was *via* Nottingham and Rugby. Our cheerful guide impressed on us that our engine wouldn't be master of the train and that if we got stuck on a bank leaving Friargate it would be a long walk for assistance. No.1532 must have heard him, however. She suddenly ground to a halt on a gradient with the brakes dragging on, caused by the drop in pressure, with my mate not noticing it in the dark. Our pilotman had now to decide whether to walk forwards or backwards for help. He was already up in the air about how useless a 1500 was. The only chap to do any walking anywhere, I knew, was to be me!

After screwing the handbrake on and giving me a lamp, my mate said to the pilotman, "The brakes are dragging on. We'll have to wait until Jim here goes back down the train and releases them."

But during my absence, 1532 had built up a full head of steam and was raring to go. In contrast, the relationship between my mate and the third man was getting a bit strained. "I bet she won't start even now," the latter said, as I eased the handbrake off.

My mate let the train roll back an inch or two to compress the

'1500' class 4–6–0 No.8538 in L.N.E.R. green livery and classified B12.
[L. D. Brooks Collection]

No.257, one of the shunting versions of the 'Buckjumpers', at Stratford in 1924 and still in G.E. livery.
[L.C.G.B.: Ken Nunn Collection]

buffers, and gently opened the regulator. Off she went. "Well, how do you like your greens cooked?" said Frank, as he settled back smugly.

It was indeed unusual for a 1500 to be shy for steam – during the Second World War these engines were used on ambulance trains for the American Forces in the South and West of England. Their ability to pound up the stiff gradients of the South Devon main line un-assisted was legendary.

Our next stop was a scheduled one for water at Nottingham. More trouble for me. Perhaps the water cranes on the Great Central were not used to Great Eastern engines; anyway, I put the canvas bag into the tender filler hole and Frank turned on the water. The canvas contraption seemed to wriggle two or three times then in an instant I had the full force of the water in my face. I was soaked from collar to boots and, indeed, had to hold on to the top of the crane to avoid being washed off.

When we started again and got under way I realised that the engine was not responding properly to the shovel, as there wasn't the proper draught because of the leaking smokebox drawing air. I must give the pilotman his due; he let us coast along on every fixed speed order and took advantage of all doubtful signals to enable me to struggle for steam.

We stopped at Rugby with only 175lbs pressure. The fire was too thick to clean it, so after a wait to blow up steam we were away to the promised land – Wembley!

When we eventually came to a halt there the pressure was down to only 100lbs. After that, it was off to Neasden shed where we signed off and Frank booked the repair jobs to account for delays before we travelled home to Stratford as passengers on the cushions.

The pilotman's closing words to me were, "Fireman, I've never heard anyone swear like you did when you took water at Nottingham, and you didn't repeat yourself once! I hope you didn't expect me to give you a rest with the shovel, but I would have made a worse job of it than you."

And before I leave my firing days to move on to 'higher things', one final recollection of an incident at Colchester. We were working a mid-day train from Ipswich to London non-stop when, as we were approaching Colchester, the brake needle started to fall, indicating loss of brake-pipe pressure. Either the guard was applying the brake or a passenger had pulled the cord. By this time we were near-ly in Colchester, so we made an emergency stop at the platform.

The station staff quickly informed us that we shouldn't stop there
– as if we didn't know that.

Before the driver could reply, I was walking along the platform to
see what was wrong in the carriage where the cord had been pulled
when a door opened. A gentleman calmly alighted, put his luggage
on the platform, helped his wife and children out, closed the carriage
door and then turned to me and the flabbergasted station master.
"You can go now," he said, "we got on the wrong train" . . .

Speechless, I left them to it and was soon back in the cab making
up lost time for London . . .

CHAPTER SEVEN

Promotion to Passed Fireman

THE EXPERIENCE OF seeing a steam-pressure needle on zero on the main line was unusual to say the least, but it happened to me! During the coal strike, supplies ran short, and furnace coke and even logs were given a trial. Needless to say these fuels were most unsatisfactory; waiting at stations to make enough steam to get going became quite a habit. The coke would not produce enough heat, and on top of this it made no end of clinker so that the fire was always in need of cleaning and no easy job with a clinker shovel.

In the small hours one winter morning I was given a job which involved changing over a shunting engine at Goodmayes yard. I had to take the engine down to Goodmayes and return with another in its place. I set off in the pitch dark with only a hand lamp hanging on the water-gauge. The coal was no better than I've described and I was frequently stopped at signals on the way. I often had to reverse the engine in order to get it to start.

When I got to Goodmayes I had to stop on the main line and wait for the ground signal so that I could reverse back over the points and into the yard. The points changed and the ground dod changed. I set the reverser and opened the regulator but nothing happened! I couldn't budge the engine either way.

I shone the gauge-glass lamp on the pressure gauge and was amazed to see that it was right on zero. So there I stayed for the next twenty minutes, blocking the main line until I could raise enough steam to back into the yard – an experience I hoped never to repeat!

That year, 1926, was an important one in my career. It was also the year of the General Strike, which delayed my exams for becoming a 'passed' fireman. These were halted for various reasons, which forced me to study the rules, regulations and so forth for several months more before my turn came to take the exam.

When the time did come it was a three-day ordeal, the first being the medical and eyesight tests for both vision and colour. Failing this examination decided one's final footplate position, from shunting about the shed or, especially with defective colour vision, coming out of the grade altogether. However, I passed.

The next day's tests were in the headquarter buildings at Hamilton House, Liverpool Street. Six of us went to the Inspector's office: first there was an oral test to find out what we knew about rules and regulations, single line workings, failures of engine and train; what you should and should not do – when you could pass a signal at danger, for instance. There were questions on the mechanisms of locomotives, tanks, tenders, two- and three-cylinders; and failures with the Westinghouse, vacuum and steam brakes with the various combinations etc.

In the afternoon we sat the written exam and of course these answers decided whether we passed or failed. The final stage of the examination was the practical test of handling an engine and took place the following morning.

The same group of six candidates kept together and met the Inspector (a promoted driver) at Stratford. He ascertained that we all knew the road from Palace Gates to North Woolwich, after which we spent the rest of the morning taking turns to drive one of the passenger trains on this line. One of us drove whilst the rest rode in the guard's brake, the positions being changed every half-dozen stations or so.

In the afternoon we were examined on the 'Appendix to the Working Timetables'. This was a book issued to every engineman, containing some 400 pages. It listed engine whistle-codes, headlight codes, single line working arrangements, and a variety of other instructions, so it is easy to see how many questions the examiner could ask without repeating himself.

After the ordeal of these three days it was back to regular firing and within a week we were all called into the shed office to be told the results. All of our group passed except one, and he was successful later.

You couldn't take the driving part of the examination on just any section of line. For instance, I never heard of any Inspector allowing an examinee to work a train into Liverpool Street, or indeed into any terminal station. I know the first time I worked a train into a dead-end, I felt a bit apprehensive, especially with a passenger train behind me.

In my later driving days I always had an understanding with my fireman that should he be doing the driving when we were stopping at a station and I shouted, "Stop!" he would slam the brake on immediately. But when running into a dead end, I was always the one who did the driving.

The Rule Book stated that when a train was approaching a dead-end, enginemen must travel at such a speed that the train could be stopped with the handbrake. This statement was acceptable on paper, but was impossible to put into practice. At Liverpool Street, for instance, a driver on the Jazz service would lose no end of time crawling down the platform at handbrake speed, and could be carpeted for losing half-a-minute! It was one of the advantages of the Westinghouse brake that one could charge down the platform knowing one flick of the brass handle would practically stop the train on a sixpence. Mind you, it was usual to release the brake a second or two before the train came to a standstill, so as not to come to too sharp a stop and jar the passengers.

They say that rules are made to be broken or, shall we say, modified somewhat, and this is never more true than on a railway. Rules had to be bent in order to run any service at all. One has only to look at the havoc that can be wrought when railway staff work to rule nowadays.

Drivers soon built up confidence in stopping at dead ends: I always checked the brake on entering the platform to make sure that it was no different from the last time that I used it, and this gave me the confidence to stop at the end of the platform, exactly a couple of feet or so from the stops. The buffers at the ends of platforms 2, 3 and 4 at Liverpool Street were always scoured bright with emery cloth so that any engine touching them would leave its calling card. If this happened, the offending driver would be reported, usually by the chap who cleaned the buffers . . .

I was now a 'passed' fireman and my next link was the local goods with a regular driver, although no regular day-to-day engine; a pleasant enough job, although the times on and off duty were a bit uncertain. Having a good road knowledge meant that I was an asset to the shed foreman in that he could now use me to cover for absent drivers.

Class F6 2–4–2T No.7001 at Stratford. These were known as 'Glasshouse Gobblers' because of their large cabs and windows all round.   [L. D. Brooks Collection]

'1100' (or S44 class) 0–4–4T No.1125 at Stratford. Disliked by the enginemen, they were later known as the G4 class by L.N.E.R. and all were scrapped by 1938.

[Author's Collection]

One of the newly-built 'Super Claud' 4–4–0s (No.1782E) prepares to start a Southend train from Liverpool Street in 1924. [L.C.G.B.: Ken Nunn Collection]

*One of the 'Devonshire Street Pots', 0–4–0T No.8127 at Stratford in 1947.
[Author's Collection]*

The more time that the 'passed' fireman spent in a particular link the more likely it became that he would be moved from his rostered turn, either firing or driving as occasion demanded. This long apprenticeship as a fireman meant that he would be confident of working on any engine with any driver on any road.

When I was with my regular mate, the job of firing was done by either of us, the other doing the driving. Drivers and firemen similarly paired were about the same age, the fireman being that bit junior in service. I took my share of responsibilities and a good sense of comradeship was built up. I enjoyed then being able to drive and of having someone to fall back on in case of mistakes.

It took about five years to pass through this link and become a regular driver. Promotion was arrived at on the basis of the number of driving turns worked. At that time the 'passed' fireman was paid an addition shilling for every one of these turns, either in the shed or on the main line but only after working 626 driving turns did he receive this extra money, whether he was driving or firing. To get this first shilling took me over two years, as sometimes weeks went by without my being required for driving. Senior men were of course given preference, especially if they knew the road. As time went by the fireman's seniority date entitled him to more driving turns, and another 626 had to be worked to get another shilling, taking about another two years.

To get 'top rate', another 313 turns at driving had to be worked, but on the main line only. If the foreman was a 'company man' availability and knowledge of the road counted for a lot. I was lucky to be made regular driver in 1932.

I well recall one particular incident whilst working as a 'passed' fireman. My mate and I were booked on duty at two minutes past midnight one Sunday in November. The driver was soon given a job, leaving me to tend the stove in the mess-room. I didn't mind too much; it was drizzling with rain and slightly foggy and, of course, I was being paid Sunday rate.

Then the foreman appeared wearing a grin. "Get on 8547 Jim, Charlie-O wants a mate – his fireman hasn't turned up. Down to Norwich with the paper train and take rest."

Reading my thoughts he added, "We'll let your wife know that you won't be home to Sunday dinner."

I was none too pleased about this. Charlie-O was one of those drivers who always looked for trouble. I only knew him by repute and he hardly knew me at all. Forsaking the warm mess-room I ventured outside into the dark, rain and mist and walked over to where 8547 was standing.

Charlie was curt and unhelpful, living up to his reputation. His only words to me as I climbed onto the footplate were, "Do you know what the job is?" I acted ignorant and shook my head; two can be curt and unhelpful. "Norwich papers," he replied. I asked what stations we were booked to stop at and he named them as far as Shenfield – as if I was incapable of remembering them any further, and then added, almost under his breath, "If we get that far. Have you seen the coal?"

I had a look in the tender, which turned out to be stacked with coal dust and furnace coke owing to the coal strike which was on. No wonder his regular fireman was missing!

Anyway, it was no use worrying about this, so I set to, tending the fire as best I could. We ran out of the shed and on to the main line, and then tender-first to pick up the train at Liverpool Street. It was none too pleasant running the four miles, tender-first, into the rain and fog.

Charlie was like a cat on hot bricks as we left London. He had an odd habit of sitting on the driver's seat with one leg folded under him – that is, when he wasn't darting over to my side of the cab to ensure that I had checked every signal correctly.

It was hard work getting up Brentwood bank, struggling to make 8547 steam on the practically fireproof rubbish that I was busily shovelling. We stopped at Shenfield, which gave us a chance to make a bit of steam and, whilst he was warming his hands by the firehole, I asked Charlie, "Well, where do we stop next, or is it in sealed orders?" He rattled off the next stops as far as Ipswich and then added, begrudgingly, "You're doing better than I thought – but we've a long way to go until we get to Norwich."

I reckon I earned my oats on that trip. By the time we got to Norwich I'd almost burned the whole tender-full. We stabled our charge at Norwich loco and Charlie made enquiries as to where we should lodge. I knew exactly where I was going; my aunt's farm, just outside Norwich. Charlie could take his chances!

He and I worked back to Liverpool Street that evening, where we came to rest beside another express engine. I was occupied tidying up after the trip whilst Charlie engaged in conversation with the driver on this adjacent loco. I kept an ear cocked as to what he was saying, and in the course of the conversation he mentioned to the other driver that he was thinking of asking for me as his regular mate, obviously thinking he was doing me a good turn.

"You'll be lucky! Jim's a 'passed' fireman, Charlie. He's finished with these jobs," came the reply!

That really upset old Charlie and he grumbled all the way back to Stratford because I had not filled him in on my past history . . .

CHAPTER EIGHT

Driving at Stratford

As MENTIONED, I was promoted to regular driver in 1932. In Great Eastern days it was usual for new drivers to be presented with a certificate to show that the holder was qualified to drive, defining whether this was on the main line, or shunting. This practice ceased some time before I was promoted, something I always thought was a great pity.

For some weeks my promotion made little difference; my seniority ensured that I was always driving, but the drawback was that I did not know from week to week what times my turns of duty would be. As soon as the timetables changed from winter to summer, or vice-versa, it was understood that new drivers would then go into their appropriate links. In the meantime I was cover for sickness and absenteeism.

When I was rostered as a driver I was in the shunting link, working at the various yards around Stratford: the carriage sidings, Channelsea sidings, Stratford Market yard, and the various yards that comprised Temple Mills – ten in all. Here was a hotch-potch of small groups of sidings that had grown up over the years, nothing like the vast mechanised and computerised marshalling yards of later years.

There were generally three shifts at each of these yards in the shunting link, which took about six months to work round, working roughly one turn on nights in three. At least I could now arrange my life for a few weeks ahead, a blessing after the 'passed' fireman's link which I had worked previously.

The locomotives used for shunting were mainly 'Buckjumpers', either built or converted for the job. In the early 1880s the Great Eastern had only a handful of purpose-built shunting engines, the work in most part being undertaken by venerable old tender engines due for retirement. One can visualise these veterans clanking and wheezing to-and-fro with interminable pauses as the driver wound the reversing gear over each time he had to change direction!

When James Holden took over as Locomotive Superintendent in 1885, he immediately applied himself to building fifty shunting tank engines, all of which were constructed at Stratford in the short time of two-and-a-half years. They were a great success on shunting work, and in 1887 one of them was given Westinghouse brakes and tried on the Enfield passenger service with even greater success. In consequence the final batch of ten were built as passenger engines.

Following these engines, 140 slightly larger 0–6–0 tanks were built between 1890 and 1901, which were the true 'Buckjumpers'. Only forty were shunters, the remaining hundred being continually updated and modified with larger tanks, condensing apparatus, and higher pressure boilers. These were followed in 1904 by twenty similar engines based on the modified versions. And then came thirty further engines with side-windows in the cabs, of which twenty were for shunting only. In addition there were twenty with smaller tanks, used on lightly-loaded branch lines, some of them between Fenchurch Street and Blackwall.

With the advent from 1915 of the large class of N7 0–6–2 tanks and the new heavier trains used on the Jazz services, the 'Bucks' were taken off passenger work and converted for shunting. This meant fitting them with lever-type reversing gear, which was much quicker to operate when shunting than the screw type.

Simple three-link couplings were also fitted in place of the screw couplings, and a number of other changes were made. Not all of them were converted however. Several remained on empty carriage work or were transferred to country runs on less hectic branch lines. So handy were these engines when converted to shunting that the L.N.E.R. had no need to build shunting engines and our 'Bucks' were transferred all over the system, even to Scotland.

There were also a handful of small four-coupled tanks, which worked in yards with sharp curves, such as at Canning Town and Devonshire Street. Here the yard was reached by a steep incline between the local and through lines and this necessitated the use of engines with cut-down cabs and chimneys – the Y4 class or 'Pots' as we knew them. These were quite sizable engines with outside cylinders and Walschaerts valve-gear. They had a short, 6′ wheelbase and in consequence swayed about quite alarmingly when moving at anyting above walking pace. Several got derailed on the main line whilst being worked back to Stratford a little too enthusiastically!

Goods shunting engines had no train brakes; just a hand brake and steam brake which acted on the engine only. The latter was very adaptable and well suited to shunting. The carriage shunting engines had the Westinghouse in addition to the usual handbrake, and in many cases the vacuum brake also.

In the days before the Grouping in 1923, most of the railways used vacuum brakes. The Great Eastern was universal in fitting the Westinghouse to passenger engines and carriages, but several engines were also fitted with vacuum brakes so as to be able to work through trains from 'foreign' lines. These latter also fitted some of their engines with Westinghouse brakes so that they could do the same.

When the L.N.E.R. came into being, the compressed air brake was phased out in favour of the vacuum and in 1924 trials were conducted with a vacuum-braked train on the suburban services. These were a wash-out for the reasons of stopping and starting I have already given.

Reluctantly the management decided that they would have to make an exception of the Great Eastern suburban service for the time being, although in fact it remained a Westinghouse service until electrification in 1960. However, much of the express train stock that was built in later years was vacuum-fitted and so of necessity were many of the carriage shunting engines too.

Before the Clean Air Acts of recent years, fog was an everyday occurrence in the East End. When a thick fog descended it slowed up shunting operations considerably; it all had to be done under the instruction of whistle codes from the shunter, as he was invisible. In these cases it was important to stop the engine from blowing off, or it would be impossible to hear anything.

Shed-shunting at Stratford was a thankless task. The depot consisted of two large sheds, the Jubilee and the New, both double-ended, with twelve and six roads each, with the coal stages between them. In addition, there were various other small sheds and sidings littered about.

Shed-shunting or shed-turning, as it was called, consisted of moving engines from one road to another so that they were in the correct positions for their next turns of duty. Before buffering up or moving any engine, they had to be checked to ensure that no-one was working on them, and in fog shunting was a slow job – we had to crawl along to avoid accidents.

The back end of the Jubilee shed, especially, could be lethal. On one occasion our job was to keep all the engines up at the departure end of the shed so as to leave room for engines arriving. We were moving some engines along the next-but-one-road to the side of the shed. The end road was clear, and I was walking along the rail next to the brickwork so as to get a good view and to give my mate the necessary hand-signals. I suddenly felt something push me on my arm. I turned round to realise that it was another engine moving quietly along the road I was in. I quickly grasped the buffer and walked backwards along the rail head until I managed to step off the track onto a crossing at the end of the shed. The engine finally stopped and the driver appeared in the cab, his face the colour of this page. To say that he was scared was putting it mildly! He had seen me alright, but as he explained when he had gathered his wits, there was so much coal jammed around the handbrake that he could not move it. The engine, a 'Little Goods' 0–6–0, had only a few pounds of steam on the clock – not enough even to blow the whistle or operate the steam brake, neither could he operate the reverser quickly enough. . . .

Some peculiar things could happen to engines around the shed and on the main line. I remember an incident one day when I was sitting in the mess-room, and a rather agitated firelighter rushed in to ask me if I would come to look at an engine in the shed and tell him if the boiler was full up. He seemed so excited that I followed him out and up on to the footplate of the engine in question.

I was confronted by a gauge-glass with no water level showing. Only with experience could one tell if the tube was full of water or steam. I deduced that it was full of steam, which implied that the water level in the boiler was getting dangerously low – something that didn't make the firelighter feel any more relaxed!

"Let's see if we can put the injector on," I said, and by manipulating the cocks at the top and bottom of the gauge-glass was able to 'bounce' the water into view at the bottom of the glass. Therefore there was just enough water covering the firebox crown to make it safe to put the injector on. The firelighter didn't hang around; he was off the engine and out of the shed, expecting the boiler to explode any second. . . .

There were a number of changes and improvements in facilities made at Stratford shed in the time that I was there. The coaling plant had two roads, one on either side, and lay between the Jubilee and New sheds. It was a general rule that between 10pm and 2am tender engines were coaled only on the Jubilee shed side, so as to keep the other one clear for the flood of tank engines returning from suburban duties for the night. Two sets of men, booking on duty at 8pm and 10pm, were allotted to take tender engines from the coal roads and put them in the shed.

Originally, the coaling plant at Stratford consisted of a ramp between the two roads, up which wagons of loco coal were pushed. The coal was then transferred to one-cwt. trolleys and these were tipped into the tender or bunkers of the engines below. In the early 1920s, a new mechanical plant was built, which remained until the end of steam. This consisted of a huge reinforced concrete structure with a hopper containing enough fuel to last 24 hours. It was filled by a conveyor belt from the coal wagons, which were shunted into three roads beneath it. Filling the hopper was a whole morning's work. From it led six chutes, three to each side, two of which were narrow for loading tank engine bunkers. The stage was long enough to position three of the N7 0–6–2 tanks, buffer to buffer, alongside.

At smaller sheds, the coaling stage consisted of a wooden platform, requiring the coal to be moved twice – once from the wagon to the platform, and then into the engine bunker or tender. This crude arrangement was generally altered in the 1920s, when the practice was to coal direct from the wagon by lodging the door open on a strut. The coalman then stood on the door, as a platform, and coaled the engine.

For a short while the engine crews coaled their own engines from the new coal stage at Stratford. The engine was stopped in position and levers were operated to record the engine's number and deliver the coal. In practice this system caused delays and it did not last long.

An interesting development was the installation of a water-softening plant at Stratford. It is fair to say that in the end it worked perfectly, although during the first six months the teething troubles seemed to be endless.

Hard water in engine boilers can cause 'priming'. That is, impurities in the water form a foam on the surface of the water in the boiler and water gets carried along with the steam and passes into the cylinders. When the water softening plant was installed, we enginemen thought that our priming troubles would be over. This proved to be true, to a point, but did we pay for it!

We soon began to notice that firetubes began to leak more often than was usual, not only at the firebox end, but also in the smokebox. Then the lead plugs also started to leak, and at first we thought that the lead which the works was supplying must have been inferior quality. This was then followed by firebox stays leaking and by this time our boilermakers were inundated with work.

It was then that we learned the reasons for these problems. The new water softening plant was the culprit. Apparently the ratio of the chemicals used in the plant depended on the hardness of the water to be treated, and someone had got it wrong. The net result was that accumulated scale in the boilers had softened, causing leakages. It took six months for the situation with these chemicals to right itself, and even longer to effect repairs to the back-log of leaky boilers.

Our troubles did not end there. At the same time, everyone at the depot noticed that the ground around the shed was more soggy than usual, and put it down to the drains. Then followed a period when we were forever falling over gangs of men with rods, poking them into every drain in sight; but despite their efforts, things got worse. Stratford depot was in danger of becoming a quagmire: the engine pits started to flood, first at the drain end, until they became useless for oiling-up. In desperation, the Water Board were called in to investigate, and the trouble was eventually traced to the water softening plant. Apparently, the incoming water to the plant built up a back-pressure, causing the mains pipes to leak into the ground.

Eventually the depot was dry once more. In any event we found it hard to understand why the authorities installed the plant when the water at Stratford was of reasonable quality compared with that say, at Southend or Harwich. Generally speaking, the Stratford sub-depots, Wood Street, Enfield and Ilford, all had water on a par with the parent depot, and engines on suburban work lasted quite a week between boiler washouts. We didn't often suffer with priming trouble, but at Southend and Harwich things were quite the opposite. Their engines tended to prime and foam after only two days from washout.

The Southend drivers had an effective, if crude, method of preventing trouble. On an up train, with about half an hour's run to Liverpool Street, the water handles of both injectors would be opened, so that as much Southend water from the tanks or tender as possible was let out onto the track, the supply being replenished at

Liverpool Street with water of better quality.

The Harwich engine crews were provided with a different solution to the problem. They drew from the stores a bottle of fluid which could be added to the tank when taking water. I was informed that, once started, the treatment had to be continued until the engine's next washout.

CHAPTER NINE

Never a dull day!

IT WAS AN OLD saying that the driver of an engine had to use all his
five senses when working, if he was to do his job properly, and this
adage was very true. Seeing is of course all-important, as was the
sense of feeling when locating the controls in the dark. There was no
light in the cab, save for the glare from the firehole if the door was
open and the glimmer from the gauge-glass lamp.

It was also important to know where to put your hands, or you
would soon feel that some of the controls were extremely hot and
they could take the skin off. A driver also developed a keen sense of
hearing so as to be able to detect any change of rhythm in the engine
or to hear any unusual squeaks, groans or knocks. Hearing a squeaky
pram still makes me look round for the oil-feeder – even now.

The sense of smell enabled one to detect that a bearing was running hot. In 1928 when the new three-cylinder 4–6–0s of the 'Sandringham' class arrived on the Great Eastern section, they were fitted
with special inside big-ends that gave off a scent akin to the smell of
violets if they became hot.

Lastly taste – which told the driver when the lamp had leaked into
his tea-can placed over the firehole door to keep it warm!

One of the driver's worst headaches was slipping or skidding,
which had, of course, to be controlled by the application of sand to
the rails. Locomotives of whatever type rely on good contact between the wheel and the rail to move the train, and this relationship
of the two surfaces is a tenuous one. A touch too much steam when
starting away, or a greasy rail, would send the driving wheels spinning

uselessly. Prompt action was needed to avoid damage to the rails, wheels, or to the engine by shutting the regulator and applying sand. This had to be done carefully, for if the motion stopped suddenly it could fracture or bend a side rod.

Locos had sandboxes filled with dry sand which was deposited on the rail-head an inch or two in front of the driving wheels at the front or back, depending on which direction the engine was running. On a very windy day the sand did not stay there long and could be quickly blown away from the wheels. Older locos had gravity sanding; upon operating a handle the sand simply trickled down onto the rail. Some of the older tender engines used hand sanding, for reverse running, which entailed pouring the sand down a funnel onto the track. Later engines on the Great Eastern were fitted with air-operated sanding, the sand being blown onto the rail by compressed air, whilst others even had steam-operated sanding.

There was also another gadget worked by steam. This was the smoke box ash ejector, not fitted on all engines, but we had one on 8559. It was not universal on all railways but I learned during the war that the London & North Western used them; theirs worked superbly, sending the dead ash flying from the smoke box like a thick fog. Mind you, the instructions near the handle advised "that it should only be used when the engine was working heavy".

Our ejector never did work satisfactorily; ashes came out in a mere dribble but it was a useful 'weapon' if you wanted to make a point with some unfriendly colleague.

Such was the occasion when I was firing on 8559 one day. Sometimes on working express trains we were rostered to work a slow goods train on the way back, calling at goods yards en route – picking up more wagons or 'knocking off' – discarding those which were wanted.

There was always some animosity between enginemen and the shunters when the train crew men used to shunt, rather than using their own shunting engine for the job. There was nothing that we as train men could take exception to, as the shunters well knew, but just to show who was boss Frank, my driver, came up with a brilliant idea. While shunting he suggested putting the ash ejector on – just to try it – and a proper success too. Ashes came out from the chimney with every beat, in a mere trickle, but sufficient for the shunters to get smothered.

It was successful too in getting us home more quickly. After a bit, the shunter could stick it no longer; he and his mates were kept busy removing grit from their eyes and blaming our dirty engine. We soon got the right away and this taught us what to do on similar occasions.

But I was mentioning sanding the line to stop the engine slipping . . . Certain classes would slip more easily than others. It largely depended on the amount of weight carried by the driving wheels, the number of these, and the tractive effort exerted by the wheel at its point of contact with the rail. 'Gobblers', the 2–4–2 type, were most susceptible because of the radial wheels for and aft.

Early expresses had one large pair of driving wheels and two or three pairs of carrying wheels. This was sound thinking, as a large-diameter wheel had a greater surface area in contact with the rail-head, and was capable of driving the engine up to high speeds. The use of these large-diameter wheels did mean, however, that tractive effort was fairly low, hence the use of driving wheels of between four and five feet diameter on engines for freight work. Speed on these was not important, but tractive power was. The single-wheeler was very free running compared with engines having two or more coupled axles.

But what was gained on the swings was lost on the roundabouts. An engine with a pair of extra large wheels could only pull a short train. On a wet day, when stopping and starting, it could lose time galore because of low adhesion! Coupling pairs of wheels together with a side rod, and reducing the diameter, might well impair the free-running but greatly multiplied the pulling power. Only when train-weights grew too heavy were locos with two coupled axles reluctantly introduced in the 1880s.

Engines with two driving axles, or four coupled wheels, had the advantage of twice as much weight available for rail contact, but designers were reluctant to use them. When power sanding was invented in 1885, the 'single' regained popularity once again for a brief period but, because of poor adhesion to the track, finally disappeared at the turn of the century. The Great Eastern's singles had, of course, all gone by the time I joined the railway. They must have been gluttons for sand.

Slipping was best avoided by gentle manipulation of the regulator so as to gradually apply power to the wheels, but on the 'Claud Hamiltons' this was very difficult. Both hands had to be used to open even the first valve port. One helpful feature was that the sanding valve was incorporated in the top handle of the regulator; this was fitted with a sleeve which, when twisted, applied the sand. But it was a troublesome device with its bell-cranks and levers, and for testing it was awkward to apply sand with the regulator shut. The device was later removed, with a reversion to the old-style sander operated by a lever on the driver's side of the cab.

The later Great Eastern locomotives incorporated many refinements. The 1500 4–6–0s were a case in point. Their reversing gear was operated by compressed air. The appropriate sanding gear was automatically selected depending upon which way the gear was set, for forwards or backwards running. To carry out sanding, a small lever on the boiler backplate was operated.

The reversing gear was superb and positive in operation with none of the tendency to creep out of gear that could be experienced with other forms of power-operated reverser. It had the benefit of being operated by hand or by compressed air at will.

Compressed air also operated the water scoops on express engines, the air being taken from the main reservoir. Initially, the use of the compressed air supply for the accessories had brought the G.E.R. into dispute with the Westinghouse Company who, quite rightly, pointed out that the air in the main reservoir was intended to operate the brakes only. Accordingly, the reservoir casting was then divided into two halves, connected with a non-return valve, so that air from the pump entered the first half of the reservoir and then the second *via* the non-return valve. The second half was used for braking power only, and air could not flow back into the first half should the pressure drop due to the demands of the other air-operated equipment.

A disadvantage of all compressed air equipment is condensation, which builds up in the reservoirs and has to be drained off at regular intervals. Water, being virtually incompressible, could not be allowed to get into the braking system or it would impair its operation. Engines of the Great Eastern were provided with a drain cock or plug under the main reservoir, but a pit between the rails was needed to get at it. With the introduction of the new 0–6–2 tanks in 1915 came an improvement in this respect. On these engines an air syphon cock was fitted under the cab floorboards, covered by a steel lid. When the cock was opened all the water could be blown out of the reservoir in a couple of minutes.

But it was a rare occasion when all this equipment functioned as it should. Invariably, something 'played up' to make the driver's day either an interesting or amusing one. A hair-raising experience happened to a driver in the same link as me. On this particular day his job was to work a train from London to Ipswich, get relieved and then get a 'prepared' engine at Ipswich and work an express from there to London, stopping only at Colchester.

On his return trip he thought he was in clover, the engine being nearly new; everything an engine should be . . . or so he thought.

The first intimation that something was radically wrong was when he tried to stop at Colchester, and found he couldn't. Luckily all signals were off and when he did finally roll to a stop, with the guard's assistance, the station was well behind.

After carrying out the necessary rules, the train was pushed back into the platform. Then, of course, it was all excitement. After reporting what had happened, the engine and the train were thoroughly examined for vacuum brake defects. Nothing could be found wrong, but the driver was told that if he wished, he could change over to another engine they had ready. The driver took one look at the replacement (which appeared much the worse for wear) and said, "No thanks. If you say my own engine is okay, that's good enough for me."

Everything went smoothly again, until dropping down Brentwood bank at about 70m.p.h. My friend tried his vacuum brake, and found it wouldn't function. The regulator was then closed and, although the vacuum brake handle was in the 'full-on' position, the speed was practically the same. The handbrake was then screwed on hard.

Luckily as at Colchester, all signals were again off as far as the eye could see along the straight stretch of road ahead. Fortunately also, there were no speed restrictions for line maintenance. So the driver decided to keep going without trying to attract the guard's attention. He could as a last resource use the reversing lever – a very tricky procedure. But knowing the road, he had the reassurance of a slight up gradient further on between Romford and Ilford, and his signals all showing off enabled him to remain master of the train.

He told me afterwards he just crawled into the terminus at Liverpool Street, arriving very late. Eventually he found out the cause of the trouble. One of the fitters responsible had made the mistake of connecting an ordinary rubber hose pipe between engine and tender for the vacuum brake, instead of one with a coiled spring embedded in the rubber, to prevent it from buckling. The connection between engine and tender was normally kept taut by buffers. Consequently when the driver applied the brake on the engine, the weight of the train, pressed the tender up hard, causing the faulty pipe to fold, so preventing him from destroying the vacuum through the tender into the train, necessary to apply the brake.

No description of experience with Great Eastern locomotives would be complete without mentioning that faithful weapon, the 'Jimmy' and its uses. The older locomotives were beginning to get a bit past it after the economies of the Great War and the depression that followed; engines which should have been replaced by newer ones were being repaired and simply made fit to carry on. This combination of old locomotives and heavier trains did not help time-keeping, and to improve matters in this respect the Jimmy was invaluable, to help an engine's steaming capabilities.

This was a makeshift device that would fit across the blastpipe of an ailing engine; it split the exhaust blast, thus increasing the surface area of the latter and resulting in better draught. Its use was officially condemned, although the authorities were aware that it was commonplace – preferring not to know about it.

The construction of a Jimmy was as varied as it was ingenious. Some fitters made them up when no-one was looking, to sell them. They ranged from bolts, syphon pipes or even a tube rod poked into a suitable flue tube, with the free end held down firmly by a fishplate. The 'Harrods' model was made from part of a cut-throat razor which was wedged tightly into the top of the blast-pipe.

The official objection was that in the event of one falling into the blast-pipe, it would do extensive damage to the valves, with the driver responsible involved in a severe carpeting. For this reason, some Jimmies were attached to a safety chain or wire to stop them falling or they were made from a copper tube which would not do so much damage.

In my firing days, I remember a nasty experience that my driver had with one of these devices. We were working a goods train from Whitemoor Yard to Temple Mills *via* Ely and Cambridge in the small hours of a Good Friday morning. The engine, a 'Little Goods', simply would not respond to the shovel. We could see that we would have to stop at Whittlesford for a blow-up while taking water. Struggling through Cambridge my mate said knowingly, "Do your best Jim, until we get water. I've something in my bag that should improve matters. While you get the water, I'll do the necessary." He duly produced a Jimmy fashioned from a steel bolt attached to a brake-block, with an adjusting screw for holding it in position.

I was just turning the water off, having filled the tender, when my mate returned with a face like a ghost; the Jimmy had fallen down the blast-pipe in his struggle to fit it, working in the dark and amongst the fumes and steam.

However, figuring that we may as well be hung for a sheep as a lamb, he contrived a plan. Fred, my mate, got busy on the fire to get a full head of steam and at the same time filled the boiler up practically to the whistle, so that when the regulator was opened as much water as steam would pass to the valve-chest. Meanwhile, I was busy with the feeder oiling the rails in front of the wheels, pushing it well under the wheels themselves with my pen-knife blade!

When all the preparations had been made, Fred put our engine into gear and opened the regulator. There was a terrific roar as the wheels spun helplessly; steam and water shot from the chimney – and, thankfully, with it came the Jimmy! We did not know where it went, and we did not care; all we knew was that it wasn't in the valve-chest.

A most unusual failure happened to a 'Buck' working a passenger train into Enfield – the terminus on the Liverpool Street line – one day. Leaving Bush Hill Park, the penultimate station, it was all up-hill into Enfield, with a level crossing protected by a stop signal in between. The speed here was generally no more than 10m.p.h., with a footbridge over the line about a hundred yards before the crossing. This was a favourite look-out post for children of all ages. On the day in question one or two boys must have had a brain wave. Could they drop a stone down the engine funnel while it passed? Arming themselves with ammunition (flintstones, as it transpired), they waited for the next train, and scored a bullseye for the stone fell straight down the chimney, to be churned up in the old-fashioned brass D valves.

To get an idea of this uncanny shot, the target was only about 14 inches in diameter and roughly two feet long. Beneath this and at dead centre but with a gap of over a foot, was the blast pipe with an orifice only 4½ inches diameter. This, of course, led in turn straight down the valves in the steam chest.

But thank goodness an engineman's life had its humorous days. Trains were not supposed to make unofficial stops, but slowing down for various purposes got by unnoticed.

Enginemen had two articles for barter with station staff, signalmen, shunters and others. They were coal and boiling water. Coal was our stock-in-trade, mostly for station staff; hot water for signalmen, coalmen or toilet attendants.

During the Second World War, when the ladies started running the railways, we were in our glory. I well remember, on the Jazz on the Enfield run in 1943, bartering coal for soap with one of the lady porters at Bethnal Green station. She was waiting for me at the end of the up platform, saying, "Driver, would you chuck us orf a bit of coal? We've run right art on the uvver platform. It's cold enough to freeze the ---."

I'd started away by then, but my mate bawled out, "When we come back!" – he meant of course when we came back on our return trip.

In the ordinary way the job would have been simple, but as often happens, circumstances alter good intentions. Arriving at Liverpool Street, I noticed that we had more dust in our bunker than lumps of coal and when I looked at my diagram working I found we were not booked to stop at Bethal Green on return. I had one card left to play – the signal hopefully being red or perhaps yellow at the end of the platform.

Eventually we started on our return trip – a fast train to Hackney Downs – and with all the moves in our 'coal delivery' well thought out. Approaching Bethnal Green, my mate remarked: "She won't think much of this coal, Jim!" "Half a loaf is better than none," I replied. "Throw a shovel or two out on the platform as we go through."

The signal at the end of the platform was at caution, so I decreased speed. I noticed on approach that the platform was swept spotlessly clean, but my mate, either not noticing or not caring, started shovelling dusty coal from one end of the platform to the other. Of course, no passengers stood there. The lady porter got her coal, but I don't think she felt the cold while sweeping the platform up again to get it! She was shaking her fist at me as I looked back.

Others got their coal on the cheap. I remember there were always gipsies in an encampment at the foot of Somersham bank, on the line from Cambridge to March. Working a goods train from the Cambridge end, the climb forced the engine to go slowly. The gipsies, hearing the slow beat of an approaching engine, used to appear, holding a piece of coal, and making all the signs of throwing them off a lump or two. Most drivers and fireman knew about their actions, so one can guess the result.

Displaced by the Engield and Chingford electrification in November 1960, shortly before the author retired, a line of N7 0–6–2Ts stands at the 'back end' of Stratford depot awaiting their fate.   *[L. D. Brooks Collection]*

N7 class 0–6–2T No.971 at Stratford shed in L.N.E.R. days. As B.R. No.69669, this became Jim Hill's regular engine.   *[F. M. Gates]*

I was firing on a 'Little Goods' on one occasion and on approaching Somersham bank, I happened to unearth from the tender, by accident of course, a massive lump of slate.

"Throw it overboard, Jim," my mate remarked.

"Later on," I replied, with a grin.

I carefully positioned it between the hand rails, as a present for the gipsies as we passed. My mate soon saw the joke, and covered the lump with black oil, as his contribution. Sure enough the usual reception committee greeted us down the embankment and, seeing the large lump ready to be kicked off, soon showed their appreciation; men shaking hands and women blowing kisses.

I kicked it off a bit prematurely to see the result. Two of them ran to it and tried to turn it over, but it kept slipping from their hands. They were gone from sight before we saw their reaction but I imagine our name was mud when they rumbled what we had done and we took care never to slow down there again.

Travelling one day on the Cambridge line as relief, we had to ride in the guard's van, as all the seats in the train were full. We sat on a couple of crates of pigeons and en route started chatting about them. Every time the guard released a crate full of birds, he had to sign his name on the label and give the time of their release, as well as to state weather conditions and so on.

He told us of a particular incident one day, when his van was stacked from floor to roof with crates of pigeons, for unloading and releasing at the booked stations. Eventually all were set free and the van loaded up again with empty crates. He was working the passenger train towards home when he heard a coo-ing. On investigation he found a crate had been left behind on a shelf at the back of the van. Not only that, but four of the birds had escaped and were feeding on some corn spilt on the shelf. He also found that according to the label, they should have been released before he stopped at Cambridge. At the time he was passing Audley End.

So there he was, in something of a panic, hurrying to get the crate to the open door of the van. When he did manage it and opened the trap, the remaining pigeons would not fly out because of the strong draught. They just flew back into the van. So he had a rare old time struggling among the empty crates to catch them one by one and toss them out willy-nilly. Of course he signed the label as though he had released them at the correct point.

He often wondered what the owner thought when the birds arrived home, doubtless in record time, but a bit bedraggled and rather the worse for wear. . . .

CHAPTER TEN

Return to Enfield

BECAUSE OF THE SIZE of Stratford shed and the number of engines stabled there, two separate crews were allocated for the 'coal road' at night. This entailed putting the tender engines away after their crews had left them; occasionally it was my job to move them for being coaled and then stable them. Tank engines were put to bed by their own crews, always using the left-hand side of the coaling stage. This was done between ten o'clock at night and two in the morning, keeping the right-hand side clear for tender engines.

This job could get quite hectic, as the latter would often arrive in batches, their crews leaving them anywhere on the coal road in mid-gear and with the hand-brake on. The coal road would then become full of engines, from the turntable to coal stage – blocking access to the oil stores, the foreman's office and drivers' mess room, to say nothing of obstructing the walkway between the Jubilee and New Sheds.

It was then that the fun would start. We would take the first engine and stable it, then the next, and so on. The more engines we stabled, the further we had to walk to take over the next. There were men trying to get to the oil stores, climbing over engines, through their cabs, or walking round the line. On one occasion, we had just cleared the coal road as far as the foreman's office, outside which was standing B17 4–6–0 No.2801 *Holkham.* My regular mate was having trouble getting her to move, and asked me to see what I could do.

This was in 1929, shortly after 2801 was built, and she had a graduated steam brake working with the vacuum brake. I understood this arrangement from my examination, but this was the first of the breed that I had actually met face-to-face.

The first thing I checked was to see if the reversing gear was in full gear, which it was; the steam brake was off, the handbrake was off, and there was plenty of steam in the boiler. I opened the regulator and muttered, "Come on, do your stuff." All that happened was that the steam chest gauge registered full pressure but there was no response at all. Thinking that she may be on dead centre (impossible for a three-cylinder engine, but just to be sure), I reversed the engine and tried once more. But again, nothing happened.

The foreman appeared at this moment and complained that we were blocking his office entrance and told us in no uncertain terms what we could do with ourselves.

Then the penny dropped with me, and away *Holkham* went, to cheers and the usual soldiers' farewells.

What had happened was that the crew had left her – so as to confuse matters for us – by applying the brake with the vacuum combination instead of the steam brake. They had then closed the vacuum brake by shutting the isolating cock and returned the handle to the off position. This left the brakes with a vacuum still in them, holding the brakes on. I should have remembered to try the proportional vacuum release valve, this being the only way to destroy the vacuum left in the brake cylinders.

One of the problems that we had to contend with was smoke nuisance. Until recent years, London was famous for its peasoup smogs, and nowhere were they worse than in the East End.

In the old days of the G.E.R., before the Jazz service was thought of, most firemen, working an Enfield or Chingford train into London would, after leaving Hackney Downs, place more coal on one side of the fire box. This would build up a good body of fire for running into the terminus without making a lot of smoke. The steam pressure would fall slightly, but as it was the end of the journey, the fireman could allow the water level in the boiler to drop. This saved him closing the damper and gave him scope in working the injector to keep the engine quiet.

However, we enginemen had to do our bit to prevent the making of smoke, not for environmental reasons, but because it denoted uneconomical burning of coal.

Smoke prevention was particularly strict at Liverpool Street, when in the rush-hours there could be as many as eighteen or more locos at a time under the glass roof. Any more smoke than was necessary caused no end of friction between the enginemen and the loco and traffic inspectors – to say nothing of any painters when the roof was being painted, as it frequently was.

On arrival at Liverpool Street there would in the ordinary way be little smoke and, after the train had departed again and the engine moved to take over the next down train, it would be out in the open away from the glass roof. Then the fire could be raked over to get it into the correct shape; pressure would rise and there would be plenty of space in the boiler to allow the injectors to be put on, thus keeping the engine quiet. With the blower full on, by the time the train was ready to leave, the fire would be white-hot, the boiler full, and the pressure at maximum.

Liverpool Street station was cut in half by the two main-line Platforms 9 and 10, which terminate under the Great Eastern Hotel. When working an express train into these platforms we were forced to draw right up to the end, with the engine chimney right under the hotel. If the wind was in the wrong direction, we received instructions from all quarters as to what we should do with our engine!

But it didn't choke the rats. I wonder how many of my mates remember the track which used to continue along from Platforms 1 and 2, right on the Metropolitan Railway? Long after it ceased to be used there were rats galore under the tunnel. It was a favourite joke with us when taking water at the crane between these platforms to place a piece of bread on the ground with the hand lamp shining on it, climb in the cab above it and wait for the rats to appear. We would then hurl lumps of coal at them.

Adam Cunningham would rarely take such liberties with his coal. Adam was one of our number at Enfield in the years after the First World War whose regular engine was a 'Buck', No.60. At that time the Company awarded a bonus to the crew at each depot who over a period used the least amount of coal per mile, and he and his mate always won the prize.

Adam was a good and competent engineman, stopping and starting smartly at stations, and coasting whenever possible. The coal tests took place at random, so no-one knew when to expect them.

He used the following techniques to ensure consistent and continuous economy. The coalmen in those days used to work two shifts, from 5am to 2pm and from 2pm to 11pm. There was thus a period between 11 at night and 5 in the morning when the coal stage was unattended.

If booked on duty before 5am, he would draw his engine along-side one of the loco coal wagons and tell his mate to get in and pass over lumps of a suitable size for the firebox, which he would then fill to above the level of the firehole. And then if there was still time he would stack further coal in the corners of the cab.

Thus equipped, the engine would go to London and back without using the shovel. Each day he would thus have one round trip to his credit without drawing on any of the coal booked to him.

A similar procedure was followed if his shift finished after 11pm when the engine cab would be piled up with coal – so as to give his opposite mate a good start next morning – while he booked the repairs and locked up. Imitation being the sincerest form of flattery, I have done the same myself scores of times, but not because of the bonus.

At the beginning of the Second World War, I was in the long-distance goods link. These turns were taken by the new L.N.E.R. Standard or J39 class 0–6–0s which had replaced the 'Little Goods' on these duties. These simple engines were built for work, but were otherwise unspectacular.

Stratford had to live up to its reputation as parent depot to all of its suburban sub-depots for their engines and materials. The fitters had a difficult job. Shortage of materials meant that they had to make-do and mend. The foreman fitter 'resided' at 'Oat Cottage' while the foreman boiler fitter was to be found by the New Shed, adjacent to the 'Ladies Lavatory' road. This terminology dated back to the World War I when women cleaners were employed at Stratford, and the necessary facilities had to be provided.

It was quite usual at this time to be half an hour or so late leaving the shed because of waiting for repairs to the engine, or for an engine to return home.

Shortly after, I moved into the suburban passenger link, which included my being 'spare' to cover for any shortages of crews on passenger work. On one occasion I was instructed by the foreman that my mate and I were to go passenger to Liverpool Street and await instructions to relieve crews on suburban trains.

We were not there long before we were told to relieve the crew of an N7 0–6–2T in No.3 engine dock and work the train to Chingford. It was night time, in the black-out, and the sirens had already sounded. The only lights visible were those of the signals, plus the train head and tail lights.

The N7 was already in the dock, which was a short siding provided at the end of the platform to hold it, after the train had left for its next journey. The incoming engine then moved up the platform and into the dock, to await the next incoming train, which it then took over for the subsequent down journey.

After the normal conversation with the driver about the condition of the engine, he and his mate left. All cabs were now provided with tarpaulin curtains as a black-out precaution to prevent any glare from the firehole. Looking outside the cab was like peering into a darkened room.

Shortly afterwards we heard the incoming train rattle by and into the platform and, after giving the signalman time to alter the points to allow me to back out of the dock, I looked out for the ground signal light.

It seemed rather dim, I'll admit, but it was green. I opened the regulator, and promptly put the 0–6–2T onto mother earth! Engine docks were provided with a derailer which worked with the ground signal and points to prevent an engine backing out of the dock past a red signal and fouling the main line. This is precisely what I had done.

Of course, I was 'on the carpet' and received a severe caution and a day's suspension, against which I appealed on the grounds that I had seen a green light.

What had happened was that the driver I relieved, working in the black-out, did not put the engine far enough into the dock, with the result that the signalman was able to throw the points and open the derailer. When I looked out for the signal I was viewing it from overhead. This caused me to see the lamp through the green glass, which was above the red one. In the black-out, of course, there were no other points of reference, and to all intents and purposes, I thought I had the road.

Twice I had to appeal against the punishment, and in the end it was reduced to a severe reprimand only.

Shortly afterwards in 1941, my wife and I weighed the pros and cons and decided to move back to Enfield from Leyton: I would put in for the first driving vacancy at Enfield Town shed.

I registered my application and a vacancy arose more quickly than I had expected – in fact, in a way that I would have preferred not to have happened. During a raid on London, a bomb fell on Liverpool Street, the shrapnel killing the Enfield driver of 'Glasshouse Gobbler' 2–4–2T No.7008. I was senior applicant, and thus replaced the unfortunate man and also took over his loco – which still had the holes in the cab roof.

Things had changed at Enfield in the twenty years that I had been away, both in the engines stationed there and in the running of the depot.

During my stay at Stratford the local Union branch was the place to go for advice on labour relations, when perhaps an official of the Union would attend if a member had to see the management about any grievance. It was the same if a member was summoned for a misdemeanour, as happened in my case just previously. At Enfield, the local branch was very slip-shod and I also discovered that the men there had been awaiting my arrival. It appeared that I was something of a celebrity, as they had been following my appeals about my derailment in the A.S.L.E.F. journal, and in consequence asked me to become Chairman of their branch.

In 1948 came Nationalisation. Most of the Gobblers had been re-placed by N7 tanks by the end of the War and, after several stormy meetings with management, we at Enfield returned to having regular engines, having convinced our seniors that this would work to their advantage. Until this time Enfield had manned only the Enfield and Chingford trains, but we also managed to win rostered turns on the Hertford line. This gave us a bit more variety and enabled us to cover Hertford and Bishops Stortford jobs in emergencies, which was to the management's benefit.

With Nationalisation, the engines were renumbered yet again; this time 60,000 was added to the numbers. I remember that on the older engines one could see both the outlines of the original G.E.R. lettering, also the previous L.N.E.R. lettering beneath the new British Railways paint.

All the old Gobblers at Enfield had now been replaced. We had the original N7s with short-travel valves. Not many changes took place in motive power; the Shenfield line had been electrified in 1949, and there were plans to extend it to Southend, Clacton and also to Enfield and Chingford. Temporarily we thus had to make do with what we had. One new class of engine had appeared, the L1 2–6–4 tank with outside cylinders. These were grand locomotives for steaming and pulling, although prone to rough-riding when a little worn. They stood very high off the rails and, sad to relate, one of our Enfield drivers, Chris Chapman, lost his life at Hertford East because of this.

After attaching his L1 to the train, he noticed that there was a big lump of coal perched in a precarious position on the cab roof. This was just before the Hertford electrification service started in 1960, and climbing upon the cab, he forgot about the overhead live wire, which was energised. He was unfortunately electrocuted.

The job of Branch Secretary at Enfield when I went there in 1941 was practically thrown in my lap by the then incumbent who was getting into difficulties with the job, not only trade union matters.

I really enjoyed the job. The men were a grand crowd and I think they appreciated all that I did for them, because I was never short of volunteers and helpers for various functions. Working life was never dull, apart from always being on the same run as it were, Enfield and Chingford to Liverpool Street. It was only during the Second World War that we learned the Hertford road and Temple Mills.

In all my meetings with management I always found my opposing numbers considerate, polite and they would never interrupt to spoil my train of thinking. Mind you, I believe we were all a bit apprehensive of what the other was coming out with.

No doubt my best success was fighting to keep regular engines for the men. The Company realised the importance of this request, but in the interests of economy they put various red herrings in the way. Many different problems were always turning up, but they were nearly all solved with a bit of understanding from both sides. Only when real disagreement was reached did the next stage of negotiations have to be brought in.

The strike that caused the most bitter feeling among the men was the one in 1953 when the A.S.L.E.F. union came out on their own. Many friendships went on the rocks. Generally speaking, at Enfield all the loco men in the N.U.R. came out with us. I still have a badge which we had made to denote by its wearing, those who obeyed the call . . .

CHAPTER ELEVEN

Working the Jazz

A TRIP ON THE Jazz from Liverpool Street would start with the fireman coupling up to the train at the terminus, and checking that the correct head-code was carried. This consisted of placing metal discs about 15″ in diameter on the lamp irons at the front of the engine. My regular engine incidentally was No.69669, built in 1925 by Robert Stephenson & Co. and was originally No.971.

Each engine had four lamp-irons: one on top of the smokebox, and three along the buffer-beam, one over each buffer and one over the coupling. In daylight one, two or three discs would be placed in set positions to indicate to signalmen our destination or class of train.

The discs themselves were white on one side, and white with a purple-brown centre on the other. At night, or during falling snow, lamps were carried in similar fashion showing a white or violet light.

In the old G.E. days there were three discs: white, white with a green centre, and white with a red centre, the latter being carried when passing over single lines. The corresponding lamps showed white, green or red, respectively. The L.N.E.R. abolished the red discs and lamps and changed the green to violet for safety reasons to avoid confusion between headlamps and signal lamps.

It was common practice for all tank engines to leave Liverpool Street chimney first. The fireman would be busy raising steam to full pressure, 180lbs per sq. in, using the injectors to prevent the engine blowing off at the safety valves.

Prior to the 'off' he would usually be busy breaking up a pile of coal, ready for the journey. The driver, washing his hands, notices the starting signal is off, and keeps a look-out for the right away signal. The guard blows his whistle and shows the green flag: the driver checks the starting signal again, gives a pop on the whistle, and opens the regulator. The 5.15pm to Chingford is away.

The driver or fireman then glances back down the train to check that all is in order, and returns to the business of making sure that wheels do not slip on the rails. Excessive use of sanding was discouraged at Liverpool Street as it could interfere with the track circuiting. The rails carried a low voltage current which was short-circuited by the wheels of the engine and train, lighting lamps or operating an indicator in the signalbox, reminding the signalman of the presence of each train.

With years of experience, the driver gets the 'feel' of his train, aiming to prevent a slip before it starts by easing back on the regulator, or he may notch-up the reverser slightly.

Suburban trains start from the most westerly platforms at Liverpool Street. The tracks from the eighteen platforms and various sidings funnel into three pairs of running lines and curve sharply to the east. From west to east the three pairs of tracks are the suburban, main and electric lines. Prior to electrification, the electric line had been the through or main line, whilst the main had been the local which meant that main line expresses, starting from the centre of the station had to cross the east side suburban traffic and *vice-versa*.

Our train takes the suburban line on the left which, unlike the others, dives into a tunnel beneath Bishopsgate Goods Depot, which had been the original passenger terminus before Liverpool Street was built in 1874.

The Bishopsgate distant signal is off, and the driver knows that the road is clear, so he opens the regulator fully and adjusts the cut-off to build up speed for the 1 in 70 Bethnal Green bank, which starts at the exit from the tunnel. The Bethnal Green distant is also off, and the fireman has done a good job: the steam pressure is 175lbs and there are three-parts water in the gauge-glasses. As the engine charges up the bank, the fireman puts the injector on so as to stop the safety valves from lifting when the driver shuts the regulator ready to apply the brake for the station stop.

Bethnal Green's starting signal is in the form of a bracket with two arms. The one on the left is for the slow line and the right hand one is off signalling us across the junction onto the fast line between here and Hackney Downs. The stations at Cambridge Heath, and London Fields at which we are not booked to stop, have platforms on the slow lines only.

With the guard's right away, the driver starts the train as before, but easing back for the 15mph speed restriction over the tight left-hand curve which carries over the junction onto the fast line, for about a quarter of a mile from the station. Judging that the last carriage has passed the restricted section, the driver opens out again and picks up a specially chosen lump of coal from the tray over the fire-hole door, to wedge it in the regulator bracket, so that the handle will stay where he wants it. The speed increases, and the draught on the fire brings it to white heat.

All signals ahead are clear and, as the train picks up speed, the driver notches back the reverser towards mid-gear. The fireman is meanwhile carefully placing the coal around the box, holding his shovel in front of him and peering over the top to check the shape of the fire. By this time the glare is too fierce to look at it directly.

The Hackney Downs home signals indicate to the driver that he is being turned onto the slow line platform at the station. So he closes the regulator and reduces speed for the junction. As the train coasts to a halt, he notices the starting signals are on. The fireman is master of his job, the steam pressure is still at 175lbs and the boiler is three quarters full again, whilst the injector is still singing away. Whilst awaiting the off, he opens the bunker flap and checks the size of the coal.

The slow and fast lines both have platforms at Hackney Downs, and at the northern end of the station the slow line continues north-wards as the Enfield line, whilst the fast becomes the Cambridge line, swinging away to the east. In addition to this junction from fast to slow line at the southern end, there is another junction from slow to Cambridge lines at the north end. Whilst waiting for the signal, a down express passes on the fast line and onto the Cambridge line; this is the reason for our train being switched to the slow line, to let this express pass.

Shortly afterwards, the right hand starting signal shows 'off' and we are away again over the junction and downhill to Clapton.

The fireman has shut off the injector, and the train enters the first of two tunnels, in between which lie the remains of several build-ings. I was told when I first went firing, that these were intended to be a new station called Queens Road, but that it was never com-pleted.

At Clapton, the starting signal has two distant signals, one under the starter, and the other on a bracket. The distants are controlled by Clapton Junction; the left one for the Cambridge line, through which the express train had been routed, and the right-hand arm for the Chingford line – and ours, is off.

Leaving Clapton, the line passes out of the house-backs and onto the viaduct over the Lea Marshes: here the Coppermill Junction signals now come into view on the other side of the bridge over the River Lea. The Cambridge line curves away to the left, gradually falling to meet the old Cambridge line from Stratford via Temple Mills, which passes under the Chingford line further on.

Two further spurs snake up on either side to meet us at Hall Farm Junction; one from the Tottenham side and one from the Lea Bridge side. The fireman has been busy meanwhile putting on a bit more coal, ready for the slight gradient from Hall Farm Junction up to Walthamstow, St. James Street. The driver has been gradually notching up, and the rise is hardly noticeable as we run into 'Jimmy Street'.

Upon leaving there the effect of the gradient is much more marked, and there is not much chance of the driver shortening the valve travel – indeed, the regulator remains open until the engine is half-way along the platform at Hoe Street, the next station, when the brake is applied.

The driver has a few words with the guard, who cannot see down the platform for the volume of passengers alighting from the train, and it is some time before the guard can check that all of the doors are shut and give the driver the signal to proceed.

The fireman has been taking the chance to add a few more shovelsful of coal and to get his fire in order for the arduous uphill slog for three-quarters of the way to Wood Street. This is the steepest part of the line, with a short tunnel underneath Walthamstow village. Hoe Street's advanced starter is almost a mile from the station, and carries the Wood Street distant below it which is also off.

Arriving at Wood Street, again the regulator is not shut until midway down the platform. At the country end of the station on the left hand side is Wood Street loco shed, the Chingford branch's equivalent to Enfield Town depot. Between the end of the platform and the down starter is a water crane, a reminder of times past when 'Buck-jumpers' were used on this line, and drivers had to take whatever opportunity they could to snatch a couple of hundred gallons of water on the down journey.

On a small bracket on the left hand side of the starting signal is a smaller signal controlling the connection into the loco yard. Upon

Jim Hill's fireman, R. J. Outten, on their regular N7.   *[Author's Collection]*

leaving Wood Street, we pass the carriage sidings which are on both sides of the line, stretching to the first road overbridge.

Here the gradient dips downwards for a little way and travelling at about 30–40m.p.h. we pass the distant signal for Highams Park where the driver shuts off steam for the station stop. Halting the train with all carriages in the platform is an art only learned by practice and more time could be lost by incorrect stopping, strange to say, than by poor running between stops. Too early an application of the brake can require the driver to have to release the brake again half-way down the platform to allow the train to roll into position. In contrast, too late an application will cause the train to over-run and more time is then lost setting back into the platform.

We are now on the last leg of the journey, another uphill climb to Chingford signal box, situated a quarter of a mile from the station itself. With the regulator fully open, the fireman may have to put the blower on as well if the steam pressure falls 10lbs or so below working pressure.

Checking the fire over the edge of his shovel, he also fills in a few thin spots in the firebed, in order to extract the last ounce of steam.

At Highams Park the gauge glasses were full to within an inch of the top, but now the injectors will have to be put on again, and the fireman keeps a watchful eye on the steam gauge for any drop in pressure, which will prompt another examination of the fire. The driver, meanwhile, has notched up as much as he dare to ease the fireman's task.

Chingford Hatch level-crossing is passed, followed by the spring catch-points which derail any vehicle running away down the gradient in the wrong direction. The Chingford distant signal is non-working and fixed at caution: this is always the case at terminal stations. A distant signal 'off' tells the driver that all stop signals controlled by the signalbox are also 'off' and the driver has a clear run through to the next block section. Clearly, at a terminal station this would be a contradiction; thus the distant signal consists of a distant arm fixed directly to the post and a yellow lamp.

The home 'board' shows that we are clear for Platform 4, and our driver shuts off steam and checks the speed of the train for passage over the points.

Working on the Jazz was every bit as skilful as on express trains, with all their glamour. With short distances between stations and passing times judged to half a minute, there was no chance of clawing back even a few minutes lost due to sloppy driving or firing. The driver and fireman had to work together as a team, each knowing what was expected of him at all stages of their journey, without being told.

CHAPTER TWELVE

Hazards and Mishaps

IF IT WASN'T the characters that one worked with that made life interesting, there were other incidents, stories, accidents, and engine failures which made each day into an event.

Driving on one occasion on the suburban service between Stratford Low Level and North Woolwich, we had an N7 and a five-coach articulated set, or 'half a train' – the main suburban trains having two five-coach sets. Each set had a guard's brake at one end, and on this trip it was next to the engine.

In the end compartment of the rear carriage a youth was riding alone. I noticed that on the up trip, shortly after leaving North Woolwich, the Westinghouse brake was going on. I thought it was the guard, preparing to stop, but to my surprise the brake then released and we picked up speed once more. Then the brake was applied again.

On looking back down the train, I was astonished to see the youth sitting on the window ledge of the door, leaning across and turning the communication cord disc on and off. I should explain that the communication cord is attached to a small gearbox, either side at one end of each carriage. A pull on the cord rotates a horizontal rod across the end of the carriage. By means of a spur gear to a vertical rod this opens an air valve on the train pipe. The horizontal rod carries at its ends red metal flags or discs. These are normally horizontal, but when the cord is pulled, these discs turn to display the red face, which enables staff to identify in which carriage the cord has been pulled.

Turning the flag back to the horizontal position re-sets the brake, and this is exactly what the lad was doing. Upon reaching Silvertown, the next station, I told the guard, who forced the culprit to ride in the guard's compartment with him until we reached Stratford.

On reflection, it was fortunate this youth did not get up to his pranks while passing through Silvertown Tunnel under the docks: we could have been forced to a standstill, or worse, he might have been killed.

This tunnel was on the Stratford to North Woolwich branch and passed beneath the channel that connected the Victoria and Royal Albert Docks. It was approached by steep gradients on either side. There was also a 'high level' route which passed over the channel on a swing bridge, owned by the Port of London Authority. We had to use this route on occasions such as when the tunnel was closed, or when working freight trains to the docks. The bridge was also approached by gradients up to it on either side, and several times run-away freights demolished the platelayers' hut at Silvertown Junction.

When I was on 'local goods' at Stratford, one job I had was to work a goods to Graham Road on the North London line, near Hackney Downs. This entailed booking on at midnight and working the train from Temple Mills. After shunting at Graham Road we were booked to return at about 4.30am. We had a regular guard on this train and from the first night, he had an understanding with me that after shunting, when we left the yard at Graham Road, if I saw the side-lights on the van following I was not to trouble exchanging lamp signals with him; that he would be in the van.

This we did all week until the Saturday, when the shunter came up onto the footplate as we prepared to push the train into the yard at Temple Mills.

It was slightly down-hill and he instructed me to let the train roll slowly back into the siding without opening the regulator or putting the brake on. I did what he asked, wondering what was going on. He then uncoupled us and we were away to the shed.

Sometime later I saw the shunter again, and asked the reason for this procedure. Apparently he had a grudge against the guard and wanted to get his own back. When we arrived at Temple Mills, he had quietly climbed aboard the brake van and noticed the guard, as expected, stretched out and sound asleep on the locker. It was the end of the guard's duty, so the shunter decided to let him sleep. My instructions had been to back the train in gently so as not to wake him. The guard was apparently seen going off duty around 11am after having done several hours unpaid overtime after we left at 4.30!

Working goods traffic was certainly a world apart from passenger trains. Goods gave way to passenger and were shunted into sidings to let them pass.

One particular night, a crew shunted into a siding to allow three fast passenger trains by. The driver, knowing that they would be held up for at least an hour told his fireman to hang the engine bucket on the signal arm, so that they could catch forty winks. When the signal was lowered the bucket would fall off and wake them – an old dodge, well known to loco men.

The deed was done, except that the siding starting signal was also a junction signal and had two arms; alas, the fireman hung the bucket on the wrong one!

Eventually they were woken personally by the signalman who enquired when they thought they might be ready to leave, adding that the signal had been off for quite ten minutes. One can imagine the ear-bashing the hapless fireman received when the train eventually got on its way again.

Harmless pranks on the railway were all very well but a more serious incident was related to me by a fireman from the old Furness Railway when I was in the R.O.D. It happened at an engine shed on that line. Upon joining the railway service, every engine cleaner's ambition is to become a driver and every cleaner had a go, given the chance, although this was strictly against the rules, of course.

One evening, a new keen cleaner, itching to drive, came on duty early, knowing the time that the first engine returned to the shed. After the crew had gone, he climbed aboard to realise his ambition: he had a rough knowledge of the controls and managed to set the engine in motion on a rising gradient away from the shed. He then reversed back towards the shed, but the engine got out of control on the down-grade and smashed right through the back wall of the shed and entirely demolished the mess room – which was fortunately empty.

The poor lad collected his belongings and quickly disappeared into the night. Frightened beyond measure, he apparently ran away from home and got another job, but not on the railway!

Each driver had the task of teaching his fireman about driving and when a young fireman was getting near to his driver's test, his mate would ask questions to examine his knowledge. Regrettably, the schooling of some gave them a rather poor understanding of the Queen's English, and whilst having a question-and-answer session during a wait between trains, one driver asked the fireman to explain how an injector worked.

The fireman started to recite the text book answer, parrot fashion: "Owing to the injector being below the water level in the tank or tender, when opening the appropriate valve, the water by its own virtue flows through the injector and out of the waste water pipe . . ."

"No! No!" the driver interrupted. "You can't say that, mate, because it isn't true. There ain't no virtue in a steam locomotive."

Unusual engine failures were always interesting, especially the one that befell a 'Little Goods' working a Spitalfields – Ipswich freight. After shunting at various yards along the line, the train was booked to take water at Witham. It was a freezing night and the next stop for shunting was at Marks Tey. It was here that the fireman started to have trouble with his injector; it would work for a minute or two and then 'knock off'. He tried the injector on the driver's side, with the same result.

They backed the train into the yard at Marks Tey, then pushed and kicked the flexible water hoses between engine and tender, thinking that they had iced up, but this was not the case. There was nothing else to do but throw the fire out and call for assistance. On going back onto the tender to uncover the fire-irons from under the coal, the fireman thought he would check the water level in the tender, in case the gauge was playing tricks, or they had sprung a leak.

It was then that he discovered that the filler lid was frozen solid due to filling right up at Witham. Consequently no air could get in to replace the water, and it was this which was causing the injector to fail.

There were two serious accidents in the Tottenham area whilst I was in the shunting link. The first was October 1929 at Tottenham Yard signalbox in which two trains were involved; the 5.5am down Cambridge train hauled by a new B17 (No.2808 *Gunton*) and another hauled by Little Goods 0–6–0 No.7938 running tender-first on the 2.45am goods from West Green to Churchbury via Tottenham.

The latter train, which had been standing at the North Junction home signal, suddenly started away and crossed the junction onto the main line ahead of the express, which was travelling at speed under clear signals. Fortunately, the resulting smash caused minor injuries only to both train crews and passengers.

I was shunting in the Yard at Tottenham the same week, and as I knew one of the signalmen well and the layout of the track and signals I had a good opportunity to find out what had happened. According to the signalman, all three of Tottenham's boxes had their signals clear for the express, and he demonstrated to me how the interlocking mechanism prevented him from pulling off the junction signal for the goods train.

Because the boxes were close to one another, there was also a certain amount of interlocking or 'slotting' mechanism on some of the signals themselves, where they were controlled by two signal-boxes.

The yard signalman told me that as the engine of the goods train was travelling tender-first, and by drawing the engine right up to the junction signal the driver's side of the cab would have been right beside the post. Apparently the driver said that he heard the signal clear, looked up and saw a green light. However the sound that he heard was that of adjacent signals being returned to danger after the passage of an up fast goods train.

Strange to say, this accident had another interesting facet to it. When the B17 was taken back to Stratford works for repair, the frames were found to be severely fractured, although not, it was believed, as a result of the collision. In consequence, the remaining engines in the class were kept under close scrutiny before a more serious accident might perhaps occur. As a result, three more engines were found to have similar cracks and subsequently the first ten were all given completely new frames of a stronger type.

The second Tottenham accident also had repercussions. It involved three freight trains travelling in heavy fog on the up goods line between Park Yard and Tottenham. This line was controlled by the 'Permissive Block system'.

Unlike lines carrying passenger trains, the passage of freight is controlled by 'calling-on' signals, except at junctions. The clearing of a signal allows a train to move as far as the line is clear, that is to say, to proceed at a speed such that the driver can stop behind the train ahead. However, during emergency working, when for instance track repairs are being made on passenger lines so that passenger trains have to use the goods lines, the usual 'Absolute' block system is used. That allows only one train at a time in the block section between signal boxes.

On this occasion, there was a mixed freight standing on the up goods road at the home signal at Tottenham Station Junction. The train consisted of about fifty wagons, including two or three petrol tanks at the rear and was hauled by 'Little Goods' 0–6–0 No. 7649. Behind this train stood 'Buckjumper' No. 7364, with a brake van and behind this was approaching another freight train, hauled by J39 0–6–0 No. 1269. The driver of this latter claimed that, owing to the fog, his speed was not excessive, but in any event, he collided with the second engine and brake, pushing it into the rear of the first train, rather like a line of snooker balls.

The impact was sufficient to puncture the petrol tanks, and the escaping petrol was ignited by the fire of the 'Buck'. The guard of the first train was killed in the resulting holocaust.

I saw the aftermath about three hours later when I passed to relieve the yard shunting engine. As I passed the burnt-out 'Buckjumper', I could not help but notice that the glass water gauges in what was left of the cab were still intact. The first train was loose-coupled, and the couplings were probably pulled tight as the train was standing, so the driver of this train did not feel the collision take place behind him.

As a result of this second accident, the Railway Inspectorate directed that all petrol tanks in mixed trains were in future to be marshalled near the middle of the train. Trains consisting of petrol tanks only had to have a wagon and brake van at both ends. This might at least reduce the risk of fire.

Most people seem to think that an express train driver is the 'cat's whiskers' among drivers. But as one L.N.E.R. express driver said when I was riding with him learning the road, "Driving an express is money for old rope. You can gamble on all signals being off and you can stop, however fast you're going, in roughly your own train length." Then he qualified this by saying, "Of course, you must keep alert at all times, because your fireman is generally too busy with his own work to check up on signals; and added danger also is that signals always being off, not checking them can become a habit."

Driving a goods train, however, was another matter altogether; there was more skill required.

But express passenger or humble goods, a driver's word was law, and a fireman was known as the 'driver's oil rag'. One driver I was with after coming out of the Army was a character about as bright as a spent match. He never spoke to me for weeks on end. He had no idea how to get the best out of an engine, and was as nervous as a kitten. He was one of those fussy individuals, who, when a baby, I reckon wanted to pick and choose which breast he was fed on. . . . His nickname was 'Fighting Mac' which suited him to a 'T' for he was a little so-and-so. He only stood 5 feet fall – wet through. On the footplate he danced from one side to the other all the time; it was a wonder I didn't cut his legs off with the shovel. It was galling working with him and I quickly found out how accidents on the railway could happen. Nervous drivers could make their fireman edgy too. Windiness, as I learnt in the Army, is catching!

In contrast, Bill Pearce was a good engineman, stood nearly six feet and I never heard a fireman run him down; very competent, but he had one drawback, if you could call it such. The oil feeder practically lived in his hand.

Leaving the pit in the shed after preparation, nine times out of ten he would go underneath at the water crane, and again if he could on the ash pit. Why, was a mystery, but he did have one excuse: his engine was a 'Buck', No. 57, the only one (as far as I know) with a mechanical lubricator. This was placed in the most awkward position, over the valve spindle rods, between the spectacle frame and the steam chest. In this position the lid would only open enough to get the spout of the black oil bottle in. Hence the only way it could be done was to wait until the black oil was very hot and very full. Only then could the driver fill the lubricator. It was impossible to see the level of the oil in it. Heating the black oil to make it run was a proper caper when preparing the engine on a cold morning. After standing in the shed all night, being low of steam, the boiler wasn't all that hot and the oil was more like jelly. Having a lubricator like that on 57, the bottle had to be heated and opening the fire hole door to hold the bottle of oil over the flames was not everyone's cup of tea. The cloth that it was held in generally caught alight but this was the least of the troubles. If you got away with a leaky bottle, owing to the solder starting to melt, you were lucky. More often than not the bottom of the bottle collapsed and you might be lucky to save a drop of scalding oil to put in the lubricator. Generally all the 'Oil Kings' like Bill Pearce and 'Fighting Mac' had their own small oil stores somewhere hidden away at the various termini.

Slogger Freeman and Nipper Hull earned their nicknames by their methods of driving. Ted Hull was a very economical engineman for coal burning.

The way he worked differed greatly from 'Fighting Mac' in that, starting with a train from the station, he would give the engine a chance to clear itself before shortening the stroke of the valve, but once the train got away, the lever was wound practically into mid-gear, nipping the beats as it were, and forcing him to put the blower hard on to keep the fire bright. Hence his name 'Nipper'.

Slogger Freeman went all the other way. Starting from stations, he would open the regulator first port or the pilot port, leave the wheel alone until nearly half-way to the next station, and then start notching up, but he would shut the regulator some distance from the next stop. This gave the engine a chance for the steam to increase to working pressure, which strange to say was blowing off pressure. This, to my mind, seemed ridiculous. No engineman wanted the engine always blowing off when the engine was working.

Now Boots Wilson had a different style: he would take first prize in a do-it-yourself competition. He also maintained that when he was the least bit doubtful of what to do when short of water it was best to cover the firebox all over with coal dust, choking the fire and thereby stop the heat damaging the crown of the firebox. This was especially important when going from Liverpool Street to Fenchurch Street *via* Fairlop. He knew that if he could get to Stepney he could crawl the rest of the journey.

There was no lead plug then in G.E. fireboxes. We all thought choking the fire a good idea, as the existing water in the boiler would be in the ring of the box, where the fire was. I bet he made a rare smother at Fenchurch Street water crane when having a blow-up.

Whatever engine we drove we were always proud of our job and tried to give the public the best possible service. There was a regular arrangement between the Loco and the Traffic Department at Tottenham that an engine must be supplied for shunting and working any short distance passenger or goods train, and be there in case of failure.

During shunting one particular day at Tottenham – about six or seven miles from Liverpool Street – I was told that an express was failing and I would be required to take the train forward on arrival.

Sure enough about 8 o'clock the train came creeping into the station with its B17 only too pleased to come to rest. It was soon detached and we took its place on the ten-bogie train, amid a lot of leg-pulling from the staff. I suppose we looked a bit ridiculous with a small 0–6–0 tank, a 'Buckjumper', in place of the big 4–6–0.

But away we went and I had a clear road right into Liverpool Street. Our arrival must have been well over half an hour late, which was unheard of in those days. (When I was driving the suburban service, I had to answer for being late just half a minute). On this occasion the black looks I had from the passengers spoke volumes but one gentleman crowned the lot, by saying as he passed our engine, "Take it home and burn it" . . .

The opposite, of course, to the train that is always late is the one that gets away without a driver. Such was an incident at Palace Gates in 1951, involving two of my mates, driver Percy Playle and fireman Hills.

The latter always followed Percy everywhere he went and this particular day, Percy went into the porters' room to make a can of tea. The train – a push-and-pull two-coach auto – stood in all its glory at the station ready for a trip to Seven Sisters. The engine was left in fore gear, cocks closed and handbrake off. Like many engines, she was blowing through a bit at the regulator valve and, as a result, built up enough steam in the cylinders to start into motion. Of course the fireman, as usual, had followed his driver into the porters' room and the train was standing unattended. Hills came out of the room in time to see it slowly passing the starting signal at the end of the platform. He ran after it like he'd never run before but as it got onto the steep gradient down to Noel Park, it gathered momentum very quickly.

Hills was quite a good runner, however, and kept up the chase. He came close to pulling down the train pipe tap on the rear coach when he tripped and fell.

The fugitive sped on its way towards Noel Park, West Green and Seven Sisters. At West Green a passenger is said to have stepped forward to get on, but to his dismay the train didn't stop! The auto then rounded the bend and started the steep upward journey to its destination. The station foreman there was waiting for its arrival, having been warned by phone of the crewless train on the way. After climbing the bank to Seven Sisters, the train had slowed to about 10m.p.h., allowing him to jump onto the footplate and pull on the handbrake – bringing the runaway to a halt before reaching the main Enfield – Liverpool Street line.

A cartoon appeared in one newspaper the following day of a train standing in the station at Palace Gates, with a large chain around its chimney fixed to the platform. The caption beneath read, "No more of these free enterprise runs."

As a postscript to this, driver Playle and his mate were suspended for a few days for their misdemeanour. Fortunately, there were no passengers on the train on this occasion.

An earlier incident involved another of my mates, named Tuffy. Driver Tuffy was quite alright when everything went smoothly, but when he had to use his own initiative things often went haywire. Just before he retired, this failing made him blot his copy book properly.

He was booked on duty at Enfield about 6am to prepare an engine and work a train to Liverpool Street just in the peak period, when every minute counts. Both Tuffy and his mate were late on duty, so not many pleasantries were exchanged. They were working against time right up to hooking on their train. The fireman, hurriedly getting down to couple up, found that Tuffy and his N7 were not quite close enough to the train to put the coupling on. With the engine blowing off steam like mad, the fireman had to climb back into the cab to be able to tell Tuffy to back onto the train properly to finish his job.

Tuffy meanwhile was impatiently watching the guard and the station staff for the right away. So being all ready to leave as soon as he saw his fireman waving to him and climbing up the hand rails, he opened the regulator smartly and was away like a bat out of hell to the next station, Bush Hill Park – only two minutes run . . . but minus any train.

The fireman stood speechless. When Tuffy stopped at the station, he triumphantly turned to his mate, "Well, we're right time, mate."

His fireman was still lost for words; all he could do was point to the vacant place along the platform where the train ought to have been. "I never give you right away, mate. You wouldn't even listen," he said finally.

Quick as a flash, Tuffy had everything thought out. Seeing the porter he asked, "Alright for returning to Enfield?"

On receiving the okay, away they reversed back to the platform at Enfield where they had come from. Of course this was now on the wrong line for the direction in which they were travelling but lucky for Tuffy the signalman hadn't altered the points, so amidst much perplexity from the station staff he had another go at taking his train to Liverpool Street in the normal way.

An Inspector boarded the engine on arrival, with instructions for both the driver and fireman to report back to their depot. The latter immediately asked what wrong he had done. Give Tuffy his due, he exonerated his fireman from all blame, and the latter was allowed to complete his day's work. Tuffy was nearly due for retirement. He was also non-unionist, but could claim representation by his Local Departmental Committee. That's where I came into it. Within a week he received notification of being discharged from the company's service, just two weeks before retirement. My colleagues and I thought this very harsh and, as Tuffy was one of the old railway servants, we made efforts to help him. After much correspondence, it was agreed that Tuffy's punishment should be to remain on shed duties until his normal date of retirement came.

The New Engine Repair Shed and the Jubilee Shed at Stratford ran parallel with each other. At the country end, engines from both sheds could leave with permission from the controller who was in touch with the signalman.

The Jubilee Shed was a 'running' shed for engines in service. The New Repair Shed, however, really made old engines that had completed their quota of miles, look like new, 'half soling and heeling them' as we used to say.

The outlet roads from both sheds were hidden from each other all the way to the outlet by stacks of coal ten feet high. When an engine from the New Engine Repair Shed was ready to be tested, it was shunted outside onto the weighbridge road, where the firelighter lit the fire so that the fumes would not choke the men inside.

It was a general rule also to fully open the regulator when lighting an engine fire. This served two purposes; it prevented condensation forming in the steam chest and cylinders, and also the steam escaping from the open cocks denoted to those concerned that the engine was making steam and the regulator would then be closed. Meanwhile fitters attended to other parts of the engine.

Just before lunch break, on one occasion, a fitter came to examine the regulator mechanism on an engine and, finding the handle too tight on the spindle, took it back into the shed for filing. His lunch time was the cause of what then happened, for in due course the engine made enough steam to come toddling out on its own towards the controller at the exit.

Seeing the engine approaching without a tender, he guessed what had happened and had the presence of mind to turn the hand points for the dead end – as a protection for the other engines – and then dash towards the runaway to close the regulator. Finding it missing, however, he soon scrambled off – no mean feat with only one hand-rail on the engine cab! The engine meanwhile gathered speed and, in full view of all the men leaving the depot and holding their breath, ploughed through the stops and finished up straddling the main lines. Luckily no trains were going by so nobody, apart from railway employees, knew anything about it. The line was blocked the whole afternoon before the crane got things clear.

In foggy weather, especially in the days of semaphore signals, trains had to run with additional caution. The service was slowed up and this meant cutting back on the number of suburban trains running. Thus, those which ordinarily did not stop at certain stations had to stop at them all.

One evening, I was at Liverpool Street waiting to take out an Enfield train running fast to Stoke Newington. It was foggy and five minutes before the off, the foreman porter appeared and told me that they were thinking of bringing in the 'fogging timetable', as the fog was closing in. I had to wait until he returned with definite instructions whether we would be all stations or not.

Shortly after he had gone to get the decision from Control, two elderly ladies appeared at the cab side and one asked, "Driver, we want to go to Hackney Downs. Do you stop there?"

I politely replied, "I am afraid I don't know, madam". She paused, then snapped back, "Well if you don't know, who does?" and strode off down the platform in disgust!

Just then the foreman re-appeared and told me that control were indeed bringing in the fog timetable. I have often wondered whether those ladies did take our train. It was far too foggy at Hackney Downs to see whether they actually got off.

"We had one, but the wheel came off" is a well-known schoolboy retort but when it actually happens, in real life, to an engine, it is no longer a joke. On one particular occasion, if it had not been for a signalman 'working to rule' a serious accident could have occurred. The driver in this case had no clue that anything was wrong. He was working an up express from Ipswich, and after passing Shenfield, saw that the signals indicated he would have to make a special stop at Brentwood. On arriving there, the signalman told him that Shenfield had reported seeing something fly off the engine and it had better be stopped for examination.

The driver grumbled, as it would make him late getting relieved in Liverpool Street. He took a quick look round and even told the signalman that there was nothing wrong but the latter was sure the report from Shenfield would not have been made unduly. He told the driver to have a look – with a lamp as it was just getting dark. After more grumbling the driver did so, and the fireman told me afterwards, he saw his mate's hat literally rise from his head. The driver then called his attention to the space where a missing wheel should have been!

The engine concerned was an 8500 type 4–6–0 and the right hand trailing bogie wheel was conspicuous by its absence. After the arrival of the accident van, it took about 20 minutes to get the engine off the train and into the siding. Then of course another engine worked the train forward.

The wheel itself was found in a field the London side of Shenfield. To get there it had crossed right over the up and down local roads, but luckily no trains were passing.

I saw the wheel after the breakdown van had brought it in. The fracture had taken place between the wheel itself and the axle; it was flawed except for a section about the size of half a crown. A most serious accident could have occurred leaving Brentwood, as on the incline there the booked speed was over 70m.p.h. How far the train would have gone down the bank that day is anybody's guess . . .

Just as our spare crews did relief work at Stratford, men who worked there also stood in for us. On one occasion that I would prefer to forget I had a Stratford fireman as a relief for my own mate, who was taking a Saturday off – Spurs were playing away. I remember this because we were only running half-trains, and in the circumstances it was just as well; when they played at home we ran full trains packed to capacity.

We had my regular engine, 69669, and the Stratford fireman knew his job, but had no experience of Welsh coal – and we had a bunker full. Now, this fuel needs handling totally differently from the usual variety from the North of England.

We had just relieved the morning shift at Enfield, and had three-quarters of an hour in hand, so I set about my chores whilst the fireman cleaned the fire. After this I went into the 'shanty' to make the tea, and was just brewing up when my fireman rushed in looking rather worried. "Jim, you'd better look at our fire – I think it's gone out!"

Glancing at my watch and noting that we had only ten minutes before departure, we dashed to the engine, and he was indeed right.

The fire looked as dead as a dodo. The boiler, however, was nearly full and there was 165lbs showing on the clock.

The fireman had treated the coal like he would the usual variety and had cleaned the clinker out and then topped up with fresh coal. This was standard procedure ordinarily, the kind of treatment G.E. engines liked, but the Welsh coal had all but smothered the firebed.

I poked about with the pricker and managed to find one or two red-hot patches, shut the fire-door, put the blower hard on, and then stood for five minutes watching the pressure gauge to see whether I should 'fail' 69669 and look for another engine.

However, the coal started to ignite in one or two places and I decided to carry on. All the way up to Seven Sisters, the half-way mark, I kept the fireman away from the fire, only letting him work the injectors as and when I instructed him to. On arrival at Seven Sisters, the water was in the bottom of the glass, but the fire was beginning to look a bit healthier, so I handed him the shovel and told him to copy the method of firing I used. That was very little at a time, allowing the Welsh coal time to burn through to incandescent heat before adding more.

69669 fully recovered that afternoon and started to show her paces once the fire was properly treated, and the steam pressure stood up against the injectors. I did arrive 'right time' at Liverpool Street and that fireman returned to Stratford knowing all about the evils and benefits of Welsh coal!

CHAPTER THIRTEEN

Finale

By the latter half of the 1950s, the sands of time were running out for steam on the Jazz service. The Shenfield and Chelmsford lines had been electrified in 1949, whilst two years earlier the Epping line services had been handed over to London Transport, together with the Fairlop loop, which was severed between Newbury Park and Ilford, the trains diving into tube tunnels to connect back with the Epping line at Leytonstone.

The Epping-Ongar push-pull service lasted a few years more. The Southend line was electrified in 1956, and then a start was made on the Enfield and Chingford lines. The masts for the overhead wires started to sprout alongside the tracks.

Steam locomotives soldiered on with the minimum of maintenance and everyone concerned must be given credit for keeping the trains running as they did during the decline of steam. Spare parts were hard to come by and the locos suffered accordingly, with blowing joints and glands, reversing gear starting to work loose on the fixing bolts, and tanks springing leaks. The N7s in particular started to shake themselves to bits.

I was approaching retirement at Christmas 1960, by which time the younger men at the depot were being re-trained at Clacton for the new electrics. Sadly, 69669 did not last the course and in 1959 cracked her frames, being then sent to Stratford for scrap.

We soldiered on with our ailing engines until the new electric service started in November 1960. Enfield Town depot closed to steam with the N7s coupled together in batches for the trip to Stratford. The driver of the last batch to go was one of my old firemen, Bob

Baker, and he later presented me with a copy of a tape recording made on that trip. As for myself, after coming off the footplate at the age of 65, I worked as a messenger at the Claims Department situated then in Kingsland Road – quite a restful change.

This was not the end of steam on the G.E. though, as it lingered on for nearly two years more. One or two of the better Chingford and Enfield N7s found work on the Stratford to North Woolwich service, together with the L1 and British Railways 2–6–4 tanks. The occasional engine appeared at Liverpool Street on parcels or empty stock trains, whilst others were still to be found on services in the country. There remained a few express engines employed on the Cambridge and Norwich roads, their numbers dwindling as more and more diesels arrived to take over.

The faithful old 'Little Goods' 0–6–0s were still to be seen on trip goods workings at Temple Mills and the docks, whilst a couple of 'Bucks' were used at Stratford works for shunting. But in September 1962 all the steam depots on the G.E. were closed and the Great Eastern passed into history as the first British main line to eliminate the steam locomotive. In fact, this was not strictly true, as March depot closed to steam a year later although most of its traffic was over the Joint Line northwards. The occasional steam-powered cross-London freight continued to appear at Temple Mills from other Regions until the mid-1960s, whilst as late as August 1969 Stratford played host for a night to one of the most famous locomotives of all time, the 'Flying Scotsman', upon its return from its last British enthusiasts' trip and before its tour of the United States.